Wendell Phillips Garrison

Parables for School and Home

Wendell Phillips Garrison

Parables for School and Home

ISBN/EAN: 9783744757478

Printed in Europe, USA, Canada, Australia, Japan

Cover: Foto ©Paul-Georg Meister /pixelio.de

More available books at **www.hansebooks.com**

PARABLES
FOR SCHOOL AND HOME

Educational Works by
WENDELL P. GARRISON.

BEDSIDE POETRY.
[GOOD-NIGHT POETRY.]

A Parents' Assistant in Moral Discipline. [A Compilation.] Boston: Ginn & Co. 60 cents.

WHAT MR. DARWIN SAW
in his Voyage round the World in the Ship *Beagle*. [Abstracted for youthful readers from the "Journal of a Voyage," with Mr. Darwin's approval.] New-York: Harper & Bros. Copious illustrations. $3.00.

PARABLES
FOR SCHOOL AND HOME

... *If Youth but knew* ...

BY WENDELL P. GARRISON

WITH TWENTY-ONE WOODCUTS
BY GUSTAV KRUELL

NEW YORK
LONGMANS, GREEN, & CO.
MDCCCXCVII

TO
WENDELKIN
AND HIS GENERATION
THEIR HEIRS AND ASSIGNS

THE APOLOGY

"MY proposal was," wrote Cotton Mather of his "Good Lessons for Children in Verse" published in 1706—"my proposal was, to have the child improve in *goodness* at the same time that he improv'd in *Reading*." A similar motive has inspired the present work.

Some one will surely arise to carry out my idea better than I have done; with greater intellectual sympathy with the young, in apter language, perhaps with less effort and so with a lighter touch. There seemed to me a need of these lessons in applied morals; I had or made the leisure for the task, and the experiment interested me. I soon found that, let the result for my hearers be adequate or not, for myself the discipline in writing was its own ample reward. I say *hearers* because these "Parables" were designed to be read aloud with the utmost expression; and, in fact, so far as I was capable of it, I thus tested them severally in the school-room, obtaining, with the ready help of the teachers, satisfactory evidence of the amount of attention secured and of substantial remembrance on the part of the pupils, who were mostly drawn from a rural and polyglot community. Hundreds of their written abstracts confirm, I can but think, the general utility of my plan; and the welcome I received from pupils and teachers alike made me dare to hope that I was really furthering the instruction provided by the State.

It would be hard to say just what age I have had in mind to interest and inform. I have tried not to condescend, which is a common fault in addressing children; and I have not feared to let my discourse occasionally soar above their intelligence. My aim has been to broaden their outlook and stimulate thought. A little history and biography, a little geography, a little science, a little poetry; some old, old stories and some new —these compose a bundle of facts and notions and illustrations which will, according to the individual, be absorbed and assimilated even when the scope and moral of the Parable are missed or but dimly apprehended. The care bestowed on the literary form, if less apparent than that employed in the selection of the vignettes, will nevertheless, I trust, not have been thrown away. The consummate artist to whose friendship I owe these exquisite engravings, has, the purchaser must admit, redeemed any failure on my part.

W. P. G.

ORANGE, NEW JERSEY,
June 29, 1897.

THE APPRECIATION

"WHAT," I asked my young hearers at the close of a series of readings lasting over a couple of years, "was my object in writing these Parables?" The following are some of the unprompted answers committed to paper in my absence, and signed with many French, German, Danish, Hungarian, and Italian names, as well as British and American:

He thought it might make people better and like to do right, and teach young children to do right and improve their minds.

I think you wrote these stories so that other people could write them, and to teach us to write them, and to be good men and women, and to think and to be honest and speak nice, and to be kind to other people.

I think you wrote the stories that we should grow honest and be good.

He wrote the stories for us to learn to spell and think and live pleasant and to be noble.

To see if we cared enough about them to listen and remember them; and to teach us a great many things, to help us to spell and to give us knowledge in a great many things.

To help us in school so as we can get along better with our lessons.

1. To refresh our minds from school-books all the time. 2. To tell us about men that became famous, and how. 3. To show the ways of different people than us, as: the Chinese, how they dress, eat and live.

So we could know more about foreign lands, and how the people do things in them, and so we could know more about the famous men, and remember the stories that he read to us.

I think he thought that they would help us along in our school work and make us work diligently.

He wrote them for us to learn how to write a story with good sense.

That we should learn to write out of our own head.

Because he thought the children would like them, and probably make the children remember things better.

You read the stories to us so when we read a story out of a book we should think about it.

To teach us to think, and if you do not come out first do not give up, but try, try again.

To teach us something about carelessness and things that teach us.

To teach us to think what we are doing.

TABLE OF CONTENTS

                                                    PAGE

I.—EMERSON; or, Tenderness for Living Things 1
    Vignette: Portrait of Emerson; from a photograph now first engraved.

II.—THE HORSE OF SELENË; or, Kindness to Animals 11
    Vignette: Horse's head from the eastern pediment of the Parthenon at Athens, now in the British Museum; from a photograph.

III.—THE LION OF LUCERNE; or, Vandalism. 21
    Vignette: Thorwaldsen's Swiss Lion; from a photograph.

IV.—ROUSSEAU; or, Property 31
    Vignette: Portrait of Jean-Jacques Rousseau; from a photograph of the pastel by Maurice Quentin de la Tour, in the Rath Museum at Geneva.

V.—NOTRE DAME DE PARIS; or, The Mob . 41
    Vignette: The Cathedral of Notre Dame; after C. Méryon's etching.

VI.—SHAKSPERE; or, Names 51
    Vignette: The Stratford bust of Shakspere; from a photograph.

TABLE OF CONTENTS

	PAGE
VII.—TWILIGHT AND DAWN; or, Personification	61

Vignette: Michelangelo's statues at the tomb of Lorenzo de' Medici, Florence; from a photograph.

VIII.—THE CAPITOL AT WASHINGTON; or, The Flag 71

Vignette: The Federal Capitol; from a photograph.

IX.—THE SANTA MARIA; or, Patriotism . . . 81

Vignette: Model of Columbus's ship, built by Spain for the Columbian World's Exposition at Chicago, 1893; from a photograph of the vessel at anchor in the Hudson River.

X.—ERASMUS; or, Equality of the Sexes . . 91

Vignette: Portrait of Erasmus by Hans Holbein the Younger, in the Louvre at Paris; from a photograph.

XI.—ST. MARK'S SQUARE; or, Sanity . . . 101

Vignette: Clock-tower, and Church of St. Mark's, on the Piazza, Venice; from a photograph.

XII.—THE BROOKLYN BRIDGE; or, The Insatiable Mind 111

Vignette: The Suspension Bridge over the East River, connecting Brooklyn with New York; from a photograph, looking across to Brooklyn.

TABLE OF CONTENTS

		PAGE
XIII.—THE MATTERHORN; or, Attainment		121

Vignette: The peak of the Matterhorn, one of the Pennine Alps in Switzerland; from a photograph.

XIV.—MAINZ; or, Superstition 131

Vignette: The Rhenish city of Mainz (Mayence, Mentz); from a photograph.

XV.—THE WOLF OF THE CAPITOL; or, Plasticity. 141

Vignette: The bronze Wolf suckling Romulus and Remus, at Rome; from a photograph.

XVI.—DAGUERRE; or, Consequences 151

Vignette: Portrait of Daguerre; from a daguerreotype.

XVII.—GIBRALTAR; or, Contempt 161

Vignette: The Rock of Gibraltar; from a photograph.

XVIII.—THE PARTHENON; or, Vicissitude . . . 171

Vignette: The Temple of Athena on the Acropolis of Athens; from a photograph.

XIX.—THE BUDDHA IMAGES; or, Death . . . 181

Vignette: Bronze statues at Tokyo, Japan; from a photograph.

XX.—THE PYRAMIDS; or, Heredity 191

Vignette: The Pyramids across the Nile from Cairo; from a photograph.

The vignette on the title-page is from a photograph of the funeral monument at Athens described at page 152 of Gardner's "Sculptured Tombs of Hellas."

Ralph Waldo Emerson.

I

TENDERNESS FOR LIVING THINGS.

WHO has not heard

TENDERNESS FOR LIVING THINGS

WHO has not heard the story of George Washington and his hatchet? George was a boy; the hatchet was new and sharp; and what is a hatchet for if not to cut with? He came upon a young cherry tree in his father's garden, and chopped it down. That pleased him and made him feel like a man. But his father prized the tree for the fruit he expected of it, and was pained to find it destroyed. Who had done it? Asking everybody, he comes to his own son. George now wishes that he had let the tree alone; but he will not tell a lie, and answers his father, "I did it with my hatchet."

So runs the story; and though we cannot be sure that it is a true story, it is a good one, and fits in very well with Washington's character after he had grown to be a man. He might have said to his father, "I didn't touch the tree," or, "I saw one of your black slaves cut it with his axe"; but he could not be so false or so mean as that; we hope no child could. He had done his father a wrong, and he would own up to it; not to do so would be to do wrong again, but this time to himself. A mischievous or thoughtless boy who hacks at things with the sharp edge of a knife or a hatchet may not be a bad boy at heart; but if he lies about it and throws the blame upon others, then he has begun to turn his heart away from the good, and will any one trust him or believe him after that? He is like an apple that is wormy at the core.

But why did the young George choose the cherry tree to cut with his hatchet? Was there not plenty of stuff in his father's woodshed to try the blade upon? Was there not a *dead* tree or a dead *branch* that would have served just as well? No, here was a living thing, perhaps in leaf, perhaps in bud; at all events, seen to be alive, and to promise shade in the heat of the day, and ripe red fruit in the early summer. The birds might rest in it and take their share of the fruit. The green leaves would make friends with the fleecy clouds in the blue sky. The wind would sound in the branches like a harp. Why did the boy Washington not think of all this, but only, " How sharp my hatchet is, and how soft wood is"? The tree was young like himself; why did not he wish it to grow up with him and be a playmate to him? What harm had the tree done him?

There are some verses which you may have read or heard, though they were written more than sixty years ago:

> "Woodman, spare that tree!
>   Touch not a single bough!
> In youth it sheltered me,
>   And I'll protect it now."

This was the way the writer felt when he remembered how he had swung from the low boughs, how they had kept the hot rays of the sun from him, or the raindrops of the sudden shower. The tree had grown into him and become a part of his own life.

I remember to have read of a tall tree in Oregon, hundreds of years old. It stood by a stream in a beautiful valley, and for ten miles around you could not spy another tree of any kind. Men called it the Lone Pine. Fifty years ago, when the country was still a wilderness and there were no roads, travellers who entered this valley steered their course by the Lone Pine. It became a landmark to them. They fixed their eyes on it and rode or walked straight towards it, and when they reached it they camped under its lofty branches, at the foot of its enormous trunk. It was thus a friend to man; and who could help loving it also for its grand appearance, surrounded by mountains covered with woods on their sides and with glittering snow on their tops? If a little boy had come along with a hatchet and begun to cut the bark of the Lone Pine, would not some one have cried out — his father or his mother or his sister — " Oh, don't! how could you ?" That tree, which began to spring up perhaps before Columbus discovered America, and was still strong and sound and might easily live another hundred years—would we not build a fence around it to keep it from all harm?

Now this is what happened to that giant tree in the pleasant valley, with the giant mountains looking down upon it, and the shadow of it each day circling round with the sun, and now and then a band of Indians or a few white hunters riding up to it and resting beneath it. A party of men and women had left their old homes in Missouri, had slowly crossed the Plains and the Rocky Mountains with their wagons, and were about to settle in Oregon. When they entered the valley of the Lone Pine, the long line of teams went forward, with the tree for their goal. One of the party who tells the story was driving at the rear of the line, and whenever he took his eyes off his horses he gazed with delight on the Lone Pine. But once, when he raised his head to look for it, he could no longer see it. Had he lost his way? There were the mountains and the level valley and the river; but where was the towering landmark? It was as if you were in a boat on a pond, and the shores you knew so well should suddenly sink and disappear, leaving water all about you; and now which way shall we row to get to land again? But if the Lone Pine was not in sight, there were the tracks of the teams ahead of him, and so our traveller drove on till he came to the camp at the foot of the tree; and there only the stump of it was left standing, while all the mighty trunk and limbs were lying on the ground. The men of the party who had come first to the Lone Pine had said to themselves, not, " How beautiful, how majestic, how venerable! " but, " How lucky we are to find wood when we want a fire to cook our supper!" Will you believe it? they had cut the Lone Pine down to burn it up! But the wood was green and would not burn; and the men merely said, " What fools we were to work so hard to cut it down!" Perhaps only one of the whole party felt sick at heart because the brave old tree had been killed by men who could not feel the beauty of it and respect the age of it, and who could not understand that it was a part of the valley and the mountains and belonged to them.

Some persons take no pleasure in plucking even a wildflower, for they had rather enjoy the sight of it where it grows out of doors. Mr. Emerson asks, in one of his poems:

"Hast thou named all the birds without a gun?"

—that is, have you been satisfied to watch the birds and study their habits and learn their names, without wishing them any harm or trying to shoot them?

"Hast thou named all the birds without a gun?
Loved the wood-rose and left it on its stalk?"

—that is, have you kept from picking the rose because it was so lovely where it was, and so fit to be where it was, growing in the open air in the forest instead of in a vase in the house? Now if any one can feel so about breaking a flower from its stem, how should we feel about wounding or cutting down a tree?

Certainly it is right to pick a flower or to cut down a tree if our object is to use and not simply to destroy. Ships and houses, carriages and furniture, must be built of wood. Then, too, when a tree has begun to rot, it is well to cut it down that we may save the wood of it that is still sound, if only to burn in our fires. Moreover, a dead tree is dangerous, because its limbs or its trunk may fall and hurt the passer-by. Even a live tree may be dangerous to health, because it grows too near the house and makes it damp by shutting out the sun and the fresh air; then we must either move it or, beautiful as it may be, cut it down, for a man's life is better than a tree's life. And when trees grow too thickly together, we must cut out some to give the others a chance to spread out and become large timber. And still we ought to feel a kind of sadness in destroying a living object, even when we must.

In old times, when men were more ignorant and more like savages than they are now, they used to think that trees had spirits shut up in them. Sometimes they thought human beings were changed into trees, but without losing their human feelings. We read in a famous poem of a man passing through a wood and breaking off a branch, when the trunk cries out, "Why do you rend me?" And as blood flows from the wound the voice again exclaims, "Have you no pity in you? We were once men and now are trees; but if we had been serpents you should have treated us more tenderly." Now we know that trees do not speak and that they were never men; but men and trees have always grown up together in the world, and however different the life of the one is from the life of the other, we cannot feel towards a tree as we do towards a rock, which has no life. The rock, too, has its beauty, which we must not mar except for a good reason; but we do not *pity* the rock when it falls and is dashed to pieces. When, however, the storm overturns the great elm, when the lightning strikes and shivers the oak, when the Oregon settlers cut down the Lone Pine, when George Washington chops to pieces the cherry tree—then does it not seem as if one of us, as if a *fellow-being*, had suffered death and destruction?

The Horse of Selenë.

II

KINDNESS TO ANIMALS.

IF horses could talk,

KINDNESS TO ANIMALS

IF horses could talk, we might not have to ask them into the parlor, or give them a place at table and offer them a napkin; still, we should have to treat them very differently from what we do now. In *fables* they *do* talk. For instance, there was the Horse who asked Man to help him against his enemy, the Stag, and, when he had once taken Man upon his back, found he had a master whom he must serve forever. In "Gulliver's Travels" we read of an island where horses were masters and men were servants, and the horses spoke a language of their own, which was not English, though Gulliver says he learned to understand it and to speak it also; but nobody else has ever seen this island.

In a great many towns and cities there are societies for the prevention of cruelty to animals. Thus, if a horse is overloaded and made to draw too heavy a cart, or if he is lame or has a sore back or weak lungs, or if he is brutally beaten by his driver, then the officers of these societies are allowed by law to put a stop to his sufferings and punish his driver or owner. The reason why we pity the horse so much and protect him in this way is because he cannot speak or cry out—he is what we call a dumb beast. He may be hungry or thirsty, but he cannot tell us of it; he may be tired with standing all day in the stable, and may long to get out for exercise in the open air, but all he can do is to move about restlessly in his stall and try to break his halter. If he is sick, he cannot say what ails him any more than a little baby can; if abused, he cannot exclaim against it. He has to bear all his pains and sorrows in silence. Often he must think us cruel or unfeeling when, if he could but speak to us, we would gladly relieve him.

If horses do not speak, however, they think, as all animals do. Dreaming is a kind of thinking; and who has not watched a sleeping dog or cat move and moan uneasily, and at last start up in a fright, on account of some bad dream it was having? Horses behave in the same way, though it is not so easy to watch them when asleep, and when awake they surely do as much thinking as cats or dogs. A milkman's horse stops, without being told, at the houses where milk is taken every day; and when all the milk has been delivered and his head is turned homeward, you may often see him jogging along while the milkman, who got up very early in the morning, is fast asleep and the reins hang loose. The horse will keep the road and will make his way unguided to the barn door.

When we come home and see a strange hat in the hall, we say to ourselves, "There is some visitor here." When a boy sneaks out of the pantry with the marks of currant jelly about his mouth, his mother knows he has been meddling with the preserves. When the police catch a supposed thief, and find that his shoes exactly fit the prints made in the soft ground as he went away from the house, they feel certain that they have the guilty man. This we call *putting two and two together;* and horses can do it as well as anybody. They know the stableman by his footsteps and the master by his voice; they know whose hand holds the reins. Sometimes they seem to know the day of the week. A friend of mine, a clergyman, who lived near Boston, used to drive every morning to the railroad-station, and the horse, on leaving the stable, had to turn to the left. On Sunday mornings, however, when the clergyman drove to church, the horse always turned of his own accord to the right, the church being in an opposite direction from the station. This may appear wonderful, but probably the horse was only putting two and two together. A later breakfast than usual, the best harness, the best carriage, the different time of leaving the stable—all showed him that the day had come round when he must turn to the right and not to the left. His thinking so was really not more wonderful than his backing when told to back, or minding the pull on the reins, or moving faster when touched with the whip.

But what if this minister's horse, some fine Sunday morning, had said to the stableman, "I am not going to work to-day; it is not right to work on Sunday"? Then the stableman would have dropped the bridle he was putting on, and run to the minister; and the minister would have said, "Bless me!" and run to the stable, and called in all the neighbors to see the wonder of a horse who could talk like a Christian, who had a conscience, and who would not do what he thought was wrong. Well, as I began by saying, we might not have to give such a horse a room in the house instead of a stall in the barn, or offer him a seat at table, with plate and knife and fork, but we could not go on treating him as we had been doing. Now he obeys us because he is afraid of us; then we should be afraid of him. And how should we feel if he went about telling people that we used him cruelly, gave him musty oats and too little hay, drove him too fast and too long—in short, beat him and starved him and worked him beyond his strength? Suppose, too, that for this an officer of the Society for the Prevention of Cruelty to Animals had us arrested and taken into court, and put the horse on the witness-stand to tell the story of his ill-treatment? Something like this might happen if a beast were to turn into a man, or the sort of man a talking horse would be; for, after all, the greatest difference between a man and a horse is that the one talks and the other doesn't.

But some one will exclaim, "Man walks upright on two legs, and the horse on four." True; but, as may be seen in any circus, the horse can be taught to walk about, yes, and to dance, on his hind legs; and even man has to *learn* to walk upright. A baby begins by creeping on all fours like a horse, and often he cannot stand alone and walk till after he is more than a year old. You may think that a horse's hoof is very different from a man's foot, and certainly he has but one toe, while we have five; but ages ago on this continent, before there were (so far as we know) any human beings yet living, there were horses which had five toes on each foot. These horses, of which we now find only the bones in our

Western country, were much smaller than our present horses. The bones of an animal, taken together, we call its skeleton; and the skeleton of a horse is so much like that of a man that these two animals are put in the same class with each other, and with rats, rabbits, squirrels, dogs, cats, lions, tigers, elephants, giraffes, zebras, camels, deer, cows, hippopotamuses, rhinoceroses, crocodiles, and other four-footed animals, as well as with snakes, birds, and fishes. These all have a spine, or backbone, and hence are called vertebrate animals. The horse's backbone ends in a movable tail, and that makes some difference between a horse and a man, but not much. The monkey you see carried about by the organ-grinder has a longer tail than the horse, and yet, in spite of it, the monkey resembles man far more than the horse does.

While we can teach horses to walk on two legs, at least for a short time, it is more useful to teach them to walk or trot or canter or gallop on four legs when we drive or ride them, or to stand perfectly still when we wish them to do so; to turn to right or to left or to back as we pull the reins; not to be afraid of the cars or of the sound of drums or of guns. A horse which has been taught all this may be said to have good manners, just as children have who wipe their feet before going into the house; who do not throw rubbish on the floor or into the street; who are not greedy at table nor late to school; who keep their clothes neat and do not soil or tear their books; who are respectful to their parents and teachers; who say "thank you" and "if you please." Children who can do these things without being told every time are like the clergyman's horse which turned to the right on Sunday of his own accord. If you ask a child why he is neat or polite or punctual or respectful, he will say, "Because my mother"—or "my father" or "my teacher"—"bids me." So the horse obeys the will of his master; but it is nothing to him whether he is told to draw the carriage to the station or to the church. The church, and the minister's sermon too, are nothing to him; nor can he understand (because he cannot talk) what is meant by the saying, "The merciful man is merciful to his beast."

The Lion of Lucerne.

III

VANDALISM.

MANY centuries ago a

VANDALISM

MANY centuries ago a little Italian shepherd boy, named Giotto, was tending his flocks in the fields, and amusing himself by drawing on a slate with a sharp stone for a pencil. With one sweep of his hand he drew a circle as perfect as if it had been made with a pair of compasses, or with a pencil at the end of a string of which the other end is fastened to a pin. It is said that a great painter passing by saw Giotto make this wonderful round O, and took him from his sheep and trained him to be a great artist also.

All children like to mark on a slate or a piece of paper, and are tempted by any smooth surface, such as the plaster on the side of a room or the clapboards of a house. A boy with a piece of chalk or of charcoal will go up and down the street, and you may track him by the white or black line he leaves on wall and fence. In school the shiny top of his new desk seems to him made for scratching or drawing upon. He is thinking only of his own pleasure. He does not ask himself, "Is this my property that I am marking on?" He does not ask whether other people will be as much pleased as he is with his scribbling. He does not know—we *hope* he does not know—that he has defaced and disfigured the wall, the fence, the desk; in other words, that he has robbed them of their beauty.

Think what pains the maker of the desk took to polish it so that all the rich color of the wood, its red and yellow, might shine as if under glass. If the beauty of it delights the eye, why should we not respect it and preserve it as long as we can? So of the beauty of a book. The printed page in the middle of the leaf is a sort of picture, and, like other pictures, needs a frame. The frame is the clean white border or margin that surrounds it, and the printer has carefully studied, first, what shall be the proportions of the print —that is, how many inches wide and how many inches long to look best—and then, how wide shall the margin be to go with it. If he has studied well we are pleased, though we hardly know why. We are displeased when the idle child scrawls on the margin with his pencil, or the slovenly child smutches the snowy whiteness with dirty fingers. In looking at the handsome desk or the handsome page, we do not want to be disturbed by the marks of these little barbarians who care nothing for beauty.

You remember Robinson Crusoe on his lonely island, how one day he saw in the sand upon the shore the naked footprint of a savage. At once there was an end to all his enjoyment. Before that he felt free from danger; from that hour he was always in fear of intruders. There used to be a time, not so very long ago, when a man who loved the beauty of nature could enjoy it without intrusion; now, too often, he cannot walk along a country road without seeing painted on the stones by the wayside, or on the sides of barns and fences, staring advertisements of somebody's newspaper or medicine or furniture or clothing. Or else, if we are not asked to buy something, we are told to repent of our sins. But it is the painter who is the sinner. He has destroyed the beauty of the rock, and of the landscape of which the rock is a part as the margin is a part of the page. He has interrupted our innocent enjoyment of the sunset sky, the distant hills, the groves, the stream, the birds in the air or on the bough, the smoke of the farm-house, the colors of leaf and twig, the shadows of the floating clouds on mountain and valley. He has been guilty of bad manners. We do not wish to be thinking of him at all, but he has thrust himself upon us, like Crusoe's naked savage. He had better have broken the rock to pieces, for he has made it common and vulgar.

There is another way of treating rocks, which leaves them finer than nature made them. All over the world are to be found steep cliffs with a flat surface, like a slate standing on edge. If there were a giant Giotto, he would surely make slates of them to draw his round O upon. There is such a cliff in Switzerland, in the lake city of Lucerne. At the foot of it is a pool, almost a pond. You look across and see a sort of cave which has been hollowed out of the face of the rock, and in it the carved figure of a lion dying in a noble pain. In his body is the broken handle of the spear which has wounded him. His right paw rests on a shield, the shield of the French kings. A Swiss shield leans against the side of the cave near his head. Above the lion are engraved, also in the solid stone, the words, " To Swiss fidelity and courage," and below, the names of certain Swiss guards who, in August, 1792, while defending the palace of the French king in Paris, were all slain, as you may read in any history of the great French Revolution.

When we look at this beautiful work of art, we feel that the cliff out of which it has been carved has not been disfigured, but has been made by the hand of man a grander spectacle than it was before, when it was only a sheer precipice reflected in the water at its base. But it might have happened that the people of Lucerne, instead of saying to themselves, "What a fine opportunity to chisel a great monument to our heroic countrymen in the face of this cliff!" had thought of nothing but blowing up the rock with gunpowder to get stone for building. That would have been sad indeed. The rock, and the pool, and the trees which make a bower of the place, belong together, and if we mutilate or destroy a part the whole is spoiled. And now what if, some day, above the lion appeared a painted advertisement of somebody's Soap, for example? Then all our grave and tender feelings would be crowded out by this rude performance, and we could take no more pleasure in the scene. Or suppose that somebody should paste a placard on the lion itself, or that there was no pool below the monument, so that people could climb up to the lion, and should then begin writing or cutting their names on it. That would be still more shocking.

In England, and perhaps in other countries, laws have been passed forbidding advertisements on natural objects like trees and rocks. But we ought not to need such a law to keep us from spoiling the beauty of the landscape in this way;

and if there is any rare or curious object, we ought to try to save it to look at, even if it might be made useful by destroying it. There are the Palisades, for instance—great columns of rock along the west bank of the Hudson River, rising straight up from the water's edge to a height of from two hundred to five hundred feet, and making a continuous wall fifteen miles long. Hundreds and even thousands of miles of good roads could be made of all this rocky mass if crushed to bits, and good roads are needed everywhere. True; but nowhere else in the world can you find just such a wall beside such a deep and mighty river; and when the first man thought of making a quarry of the Palisades, did he not shrink back and say, "No, no; we must keep this glorious wall as nature built it forever. We will get stone for our roads elsewhere. This is what Henry Hudson saw when he sailed up the river which no white man had discovered before him, and to which his name was rightly given; this is what even the Indians must have admired before Hudson came, as they paddled along it in their canoes"? Well, if one man so felt, others there were who cared more for money than for beauty or for history. "Henry Hudson in his ship the *Half-Moon*, the native Indians in their birch-bark canoes, are dead; and why need we trouble ourselves about them? The Palisades have made the Hudson River famous, so that people come all the way from Europe to visit them; but theirs is a foolish curiosity." So thought these quarrymen, and began their ugly gashes in the gray wall, which now can never be as beautiful again, even if the greater part of it be saved. They would, we may be sure, not spare the Natural Bridge in Virginia—a great stone arch worn out by the river now passing under it, and celebrated as having been visited and climbed by George Washington. Yes, indeed; who would trust them to keep their pickaxes away from the Swiss lion of Lucerne, or from the wall-paintings of Giotto himself?

Jean-Jacques Rousseau.

IV

PROPERTY.

IF you will look at

PROPERTY

IF you will look at the map of Europe you will find there Switzerland, famous for its Alps. These are the highest mountains in Europe, though Switzerland is one of the smallest European countries, being only about twice as large as New Jersey. It is a republic, or, in other words, a country without a king; and it is also a country without a language. The inhabitants of Switzerland do not speak Swiss, as the people of England speak English. There is a French Switzerland and a German Switzerland, and in some parts of the country bordering on Italy the people speak Italian.

It was in French Switzerland, nearly two hundred years ago, that a gentleman and two little boy cousins were setting out a walnut tree on a terrace. And what is a terrace? It is a kind of grassy bank with a level top, on which one may walk or sit in the open air and enjoy the view. Flowers and trees will not be out of place there. This Swiss gentleman had a bench on which he liked to sit on summer days, and in order to shade it from the sun he said to himself, "I will plant a walnut tree beside it, and the little boys shall help me." One of the boys, who afterwards became a great French writer, was named Jean-Jacques, or, as we should say in English, John-James. The hole for the tree was dug, and John-James and his cousin skipped along beside the wheelbarrow in which the tree was carried to the spot; they kept the tree from falling while the gardener covered the roots with earth until the hole was quite filled up and the tree could stand upright of itself. Then a sort of basin was made around the foot of the tree to hold the water which was to feed the roots.

That was a great day for the boys, their Arbor Day; but—the *tree* was not theirs. So nothing would satisfy them till they had planted a willow tree some eight or ten feet from the walnut, with its basin too around it to catch the water. But where was the water to come from? Even for the walnut tree it had to be brought a long distance. Then the cousins put their heads together and presently dug a little tunnel leading down from the walnut basin to their own basin. But the top caved in and choked up the passage. Then they lined the tunnel with boards and covered it over with earth, and put a grating at the upper end to keep it from choking; and now every time the walnut tree was watered, what a joy it was for the boys to see the foot of their willow —their *own* willow—grow wet! They fairly danced with glee.

Well, it was not very long before the good gentleman noticed that the water he poured into the walnut basin did not stay there, but quickly disappeared. The ground could not have drunk it up so fast; he began to look around. What makes our boys so happy? and what means that little slip of a willow three yards off, and this line of fresh dirt leading from the walnut to the willow? The Swiss gentleman said nothing, but got a pickaxe and tore open the boards, crying, with each stroke, "An aqueduct! an aqueduct!" until the tunnel was in ruins and he had destroyed even the willow tree. He did not scold the boys, for he was more amused than he was angry; and he had been a boy himself. Still, they had been taking what did not belong to them. It was only water? Yes, but it was *his* water. He had brought it to the tree with much trouble and perhaps some expense.

Such merry boys, at play all day long in the sunshine in sight of those grand snow-capped Alps of Switzerland—we should not like to say they *stole* their water, like a thief. They knew that they were doing wrong, or why did they cover over their aqueduct?—why not make an open ditch? If it had been the walnut tree—yes, or the gardener's watering-pot—they carried off instead of the water, then surely they would have felt that they were taking what did not belong to them. And if other little boys had planted another tree, and secretly built an aqueduct from the willow basin to *their* basin, then no doubt John-James and his cousin would have said to them, "You have no right to take our property"—meaning their water.

There are a great many kinds of property—for example, books. I used to see boys write on the covers of their geographies or arithmetics—

> "Steal not this book for fear of shame,
> For here you see the owner's name."

And the owner of a fine library often pastes on the cover of each book a book-plate, with his name engraved upon it. But we must not think that the owner's *name* makes anything his property. You can easily put a name on a book or a tool or an umbrella or a handkerchief or the front-door of a house, but the book and the tool and the umbrella and the handkerchief and the house must belong to somebody before he puts his mark or his name on it; and if he does not choose to put his name on it, it is still his property. The name will help him to find it and claim it if it is lost—that is all. On chairs, tables, beds, carpets, dinner-plates, shoes, dresses, and a thousand other things it is not easy to put the owner's name; and to take them from the owner without his consent is certainly stealing.

John-James might have had a dog given him and raised it from a puppy, feeding it and making a kennel for it. One day, when out walking with the dog at his heels, some other boy might have whistled to it, caught it and refused to give it back. "But," cries John-James, "it is *my* dog." "But," says the thief, "he has no collar." The thief is wrong and John-James is right. The collar makes no difference in the ownership. A pickpocket who should take a handkerchief from your coat and be arrested by the policeman who saw him, would not be let off by the judge on showing that the handkerchief was not marked. The thief only wants an excuse. If the property is not marked, he asks, "How did I know it belonged to you?" If it is marked, he says, "You were not looking."

Well, we cannot always be watching our property, any more than we can be always using it. Sometimes it happens that we own a house which we cannot occupy or let others occupy. We built it ourselves, or we bought it, and when we wish to sell it we can show that it is our property and that we have a right to sell it. Now, it is shut up and we have gone away, leaving no watchman there. We hope that it will be unharmed unless by accident. Along comes a boy, however, who is not a bad boy, but who likes the jingle of broken glass; he passes by the empty house after dark; nobody is looking and he flings a stone at a window and then runs away. Another boy, next day, sees the holes in the panes and flings more stones, until there is not a whole pane in the house. When we return, we find we have been robbed of all this glass, which it will cost us a great deal of money to mend, and the rain and the snow have beaten in and spoiled the paper and the ceilings and the furniture; and that calls for more money. It is just as if the boys who threw the stones had put their hands in our pockets and stolen our purses. They had been taught, "Thou shalt not steal," and they would never have taken our purses; but they did not see that by making us spend money without our consent and against our will, they were really robbing us of it and making us so much the poorer.

Just so it is when a scholar injures or destroys

a book. The law says that then his parents must pay the school the price of a new one, and this money is as much of a loss to them as if a thief had taken it from them. Perhaps they will say to the child, " The money we have to pay for the book you destroyed, would have bought you a new pair of mittens; now you must go without any this winter, or wear your old ones." Then the child will see that, after all, he has been robbing himself. And if John-James's aqueduct had gone undiscovered and the walnut tree had died for want of water, then not only his uncle but he himself never could have sat under its shade upon the terrace in summer, or gathered its fruit in the autumn.

Notre Dame de Paris.

V

THE MOB.

WHEN school is opened

THE MOB

WHEN school is opened or when it is dismissed, I see the boys and girls file in and out. The teacher gives the word, and they go quietly and in order each one to his seat or to the playground. You might think them soldiers, and the teacher an officer. "Attention!" cries the captain; "forward, march!" and the company, or the regiment, or the great army itself, moves on without confusion. Almost all of you have seen soldiers on the march in some peaceful procession, but none of you have ever seen them in battle, and I hope you never may. In battle too they do as they are told—they obey orders; but sometimes it happens that they are beaten by the enemy and are forced to retreat. The captain may wave his sword and cry "Forward!" but they do not dare to go forward lest they be shot down; or the captain himself has been killed, and there is nobody to tell them what to do, nor any one whom they will obey. A great fear—what is called a panic—seizes on them all, and the retreat becomes a rout: each man thinks only of himself and how he shall save his life; they throw down their guns and their knapsacks, they get in each other's way—the road is blocked, the narrow bridge is blocked—all shout together, and push each other, and trample upon or ride over each other, or crowd each other into the water. It is terrible. The army is no longer an army, it has become a *mob*.

So it might be in school. If the building should catch fire, or if only some thoughtless boy cried "Fire!" and made the scholars think it was really so, then there might be a mad rush for the door and the stairs; all could not get out at once or down at once; there would be a jam. The smallest and the weakest would be crushed or even smothered to death; those who fell would be trodden on, perhaps killed. If all got out alive, it would be with torn clothes, scratches, bruises, and very likely broken bones. Had they obeyed their captain, the teacher, they would have gone out one by one or two by two, in half the time, and nobody would have been hurt. Had they stopped to think, they would have said to themselves, "The door is only three feet wide, and was meant for one person to pass through at a time; or, it is six feet wide, for two to pass. If forty or fifty of us try to get through together, the doorway will be choked; no one can get out, and while we are struggling with one another, we may all be burnt up."

But mobs do not think; if they did, they would not be mobs. A frightened flock of sheep does not think when it runs first in this direction after one leader, then in that after another. The horse, like little boys and girls, is generally a sensible animal; he thinks, and he learns to obey. A light touch of the reins or a word spoken to him makes him go as we wish. He is a soldier. But let him be frightened on the road by a piece of paper or by the cars, a panic seizes him and off he bolts. He minds no longer the reins or the driver's voice; he ceases to be a soldier. His running away startles other horses along the road, and they too cease to think and to obey, and then there is a mob of horses. Travellers on the great Plains of the West, before there were any railroads, used to fasten their horses at night so as to keep them from straying off from the camp. Often the Indians would come up in the dark and frighten the horses, and when these had broken loose would catch them and steal them. This was called stampeding them.

One of the reasons why we send children to school is to keep them from turning into a mob, and from being stampeded like horses and cattle. The more ignorant we are, the more easily we are frightened; and when we are frightened and in fear of our lives, we often behave more like savage beasts than like men. In the year 1832 the cholera broke out in Paris, and thousands died of it. It was then a new and strange disease, and everybody was made cowardly by it. No one understood, as we do now, what caused it or how it could be cured or prevented. The poorest people in that great city were terror-stricken. When so many died and so few recovered, they were ready to believe any rumor that came to their ears. Some said, "We are all being poisoned," and it was really believed that men went about poisoning the water in the public drinking-fountains. Others said, "And the doctors in the hospitals have too many patients to attend to; some they try to cure, and the rest they poison to get rid of them." Then everybody was on the lookout for poisoners.

You may read some day a story of these cholera times in Paris, written by a Frenchman. It tells of an unfortunate man suspected and accused of being a poisoner. He denies it, but it is of no use. They try to seize him in a shop and he breaks loose and runs into the street—into the square. They run after him, and now a great crowd gathers about him. Do they hold him till they can call the police to arrest him and take him before the judge to be tried, and punished if found guilty? No, this is a mob, and it already believes the man guilty and is going to punish him without a trial. It means to kill him just as if he were a mad dog. Men and women strike him as he comes near them, or throw things at him, even their wooden shoes, and by and bye, though a giant, he falls down and is trampled to death by the cruel mob. All this takes place on an island in the River Seine, in front of the great church of Notre Dame. A part of the mob drags the body to one of the bridges and tosses it over into the water. Another part has already found another victim. It is a priest who knew the man they were murdering, and cried out, " He is innocent!" " You too are a poisoner," they replied, and they began to beat and to stone him also. He runs from them to the church, but he cannot get in, and he stands with his back to the wall, more dead than alive. What can save him from falling, from being kicked and trodden to death, from being thrown into the dark river?

Suddenly a door near him is opened; another priest seizes him and pulls him in, and the door is closed. Gabriel is the name of this saviour, and he has just time to get the poor man behind a low railing, where he falls helpless, when the mob bursts in the door and rushes upon them. Gabriel tries to talk to them and excite their pity. They hear him, but his words have no effect upon them. At last Gabriel bids the leader of the mob come inside the railing, points to the fallen body of the priest, and says, "Now kill him!" The man shrinks back. "What, I alone kill him!" He refuses and the priest is saved. No one in the mob can be found to do *by himself* what all together would do.

Shall we go with the mob and do what it does, and think we are doing right because others are doing the same thing? Both men and children sometimes act that way. Yet if any one of you had a toy or a knife or any article that he prized, would he give it up more willingly because a *dozen* boys told him they meant to take it from him, than because only *one* did? Could one boy be a thief if he alone took it, and not a thief if he got eleven others to join him in taking it from you against your will?

Here are some verses by an English poet, William Cowper, which fit the case exactly:

"A youngster at school, more sedate than the rest,
 Had once his integrity put to the test:
 His comrades had plotted an orchard to rob,
 And asked him to go and assist in the job.

THE MOB

"He was shocked, sir, like you, and answered, 'Oh, no!
What! rob our good neighbor! I pray you don't go;
Besides, the man's poor, his orchard's his bread;
Then think of his children, for they must be fed.'

"'You speak very fine, and you look very grave,
But apples we want, and apples we'll have;
If you will go with us, you shall have a share,
If not, you shall have neither apple nor pear.'

"They spoke, and Tom pondered—'I see they will go;
Poor man! what a pity to injure him so!
Poor man! I would save him his fruit if I could,
But staying behind will do him no good.

"'If the matter depended alone upon me,
His apples might hang till they dropped from the tree;
But since they will take them, I think I'll go too,—
He will lose none by me, though I get a few.'

"His scruples thus silenced, Tom felt more at ease,
And went with his comrades the apples to seize;
He blamed and protested, but joined in the plan:
He shared in the plunder, but pitied the man."

Tom, you see, had a conscience; it was his captain. It told him that to take his neighbor's fruit was stealing. Tom would have obeyed if he had been let alone. But the mob came to him, and he forgot his duty to his captain, and began to invent excuses for stealing in company. Then, as the old saying is, he followed the multitude to do evil.

William Shakspere.

VI

NAMES.

WHAT do we mean

NAMES

WHAT do we mean when we speak of a French language, an English language, a German language, and so on? We mean that in France, England, and Germany people give different names to the same thing. All these countries have railroads, for example, but each one has its own word for this sort of highway. If we search in a French dictionary for *Railroad*, we cannot find it at all, either under the letter R or any other letter. It would, however, be foolish to conclude from this that there are no railroads in France. The French have the *thing* although they give it another name.

It is somewhat so even with places. On an Italian map of Italy you will look in vain for the cities which we call Rome, Naples, Florence, Leghorn, Venice, Milan, Genoa, Turin; on a German map of Germany for Munich, Mentz, Frankfort, Cologne, Hanover; on a Belgian map of Belgium for Antwerp or Ghent; on a French map of France for Lyons or Marseilles. The native spelling is not exactly the same as the English spelling on English maps of those countries, and sometimes it is so unlike that we can hardly recognize it. Still, the moment we begin to describe the cities I have mentioned—as, Rome by its great church of St. Peter's, or Naples by its beautiful bay and the neighboring volcano of Vesuvius, or Venice by its canals—then we perceive that the same place is meant by all the variety of names.

Think, again, of the great number of names which one person may answer to as he grows up. There is the baby's pet name; there is the Christian name, of the boy Thomas, shortened to Tom and then lengthened to Tommy, or of the girl Elizabeth, Lizzie, and Betty; there is the school nickname; and lastly there is the surname, or family name, as, Wilson or Baker. If some one saw a boy break a pane of glass with his ball, and went and told the owner that Tom Wilson did it, do you suppose Tom would get off by saying that his name was *Thomas* Wilson? No, the owner does not care what his name is; he wants to find the person who threw that ball.

Shakspere says truly that

"A rose
By any other name would smell as sweet."

For the same reason, any ill-smelling flower would be just as disagreeable if called a rose. Nevertheless, people are all the time trying to make unpleasant things pleasant, or evil things good, by a mere change of name. I once read to some children a story about stealing: it was a dog that had been taken from its owner. I noticed that one of my little hearers, on writing down what I had read, used the word *hooked* instead of *stolen:* the dog had been "hooked." Then I remembered that when I was a boy we used the same word, and I am ashamed to say that we used it when we ourselves did the stealing. Did we call each other thieves? Oh dear no; the name *thief* goes with the name *stealing*, and we only "hooked." This bad reasoning actually made us feel innocent, as if nobody had suffered any wrong at our hands; but we did not like it if any one "hooked" our own knife or pencil or apple.

Boys who play truant, making their parents believe they have been to school when they have really gone fishing or idling, have a similar word: they call it playing *hookey*. Hookey and truancy amount to the same thing. There is the vacant desk at school—the interrupted lessons—the deceiving of parents and teacher about the cause of the boy's absence; but oh if we can only call it "hookey"! There is no law against playing hookey—is there? The truant officer knows and cares nothing about that: his business is to catch truants—isn't it?

Some of you may have read the Declaration of Independence, which was our forefathers' excuse for going to war with England. "All men," they said, "were created equal," and had an equal right to life, liberty, and the pursuit of happiness. They did not really believe this, because at that time they were forcing thousands of black people to work for them for nothing. If they had believed it, they would have given these slaves their freedom. When the Revolution was over, and the colonies were no longer under British rule, the same men who made the Declaration of Independence made a Constitution for the United States. There was to be a Congress consisting of Senate and House of Representatives; and the States would be represented in the House according to population—the more people, the more Representatives. The Southern States, which held the greatest number of slaves and had the smallest number of freemen, said they would not come into the Union if their slaves were not counted in with their free population. This was agreed to, but our forefathers, remembering the Declaration of Independence, were ashamed to put the word *slaves* in the Constitution, so they spoke of them as "all other persons" than free persons. Then, as the Southern States wanted more slaves and were bringing them from Africa, they said the Constitution must allow the slave trade to go on for twenty years. But again they were ashamed to mention slave or slave trade in the Constitution; so instead of slaves they said "such persons," and instead of slave trade they said "migration or importation." Finally, as the slaves had a habit of running away in order to be free, the Southern States said the Constitution must provide for sending them back when caught. So it did, but the slaves were now called "persons held to service or labor."

This was all very fine; but though you could not find the words Slave or Slavery or Slave Trade in the Constitution, any more than you could find Railroad in a French dictionary, still the *thing* was there, and our fathers were only trying to deceive themselves and other people with names. The slaveholders used to speak of slavery as their "domestic institution" or their "peculiar institution"; and what could there be wicked or cruel in an "institution," or what right had anybody to meddle with it—that is, to say that the slaves ought to be free? Now that slavery has been abolished, we may call it by its right name, and nobody cares.

What we call a silver dollar is really only a fifty-cent piece. The United States Government will, it is true, receive it in payment of postage-stamps or of taxes as if it were a gold dollar; but if you were to send a gold dollar out of the country—say, to Germany—and the Government should wish to buy it back, it would have to pay the German holder of it two silver dollars instead of one. The fifty-cent dollar has been called "the dollar of the fathers," because it somewhat resembles the silver dollar in circulation fifty years ago, though worth only half as much; for silver is very much more plentiful, and therefore cheaper, than it used to be. Persons who like this name and want the Government to go on making fifty-cent dollars, would not be pleased to have their milkman give them their milk in a pint measure, even if the pint measure had written on it "The Quart of the Fathers." They would say, "You may call your measure what you please; you have given me only a pint of milk, and I shall pay you only for a pint."

We must be on our guard against people who play tricks with the dictionary. Take a simple word like *industry:* it means labor of any kind. There is the farming industry, the shipping industry, the mining industry, the manufacturing industry, etc. Or take the simple word *protection:* it means a shielding from harm. Now we hear a great deal about " Protection to American industry," and you would suppose that every laboring man was to be shielded from harm (whatever the harm may be). Not at all; you will find that it is only *some* industries and *some* industrious men. For instance, copper is a very useful metal found in the earth in many countries, and to be got out only by the greatest industry. There are immense deposits of it on the shores of Lake Superior. Well, a few years ago, while some industrious Americans were mining this Lake Superior copper ore, other Americans, just as industrious, were bringing ores in ships from foreign countries (like Chile in South America), and still other industrious Americans were smelting these ores—that is, extracting the pure copper. Should they not *all* be protected? No. The owners of the American copper mines got the Government to lay a tax on all ores imported into the country. What happened? The American smelters could not sell their copper as cheaply as before, and had to give up their business. Then the American shippers who brought the foreign ores to them had to go out of *that* business. Did the smelters and the shippers enjoy being " protected "? No more than our British forefathers enjoyed the protection of their Roman conquerors. " The Romans," said they, " usurp power under false names; they make a desert and call it peace!"

Twilight and Dawn.

VII

PERSONIFICATION.

IT is hard to define

PERSONIFICATION

IT is hard to define Poetry, and to tell just how it differs from Prose. Wordsworth, for instance, says—

> "The Moon doth with delight
> Look round her when the heavens are bare,"

—as if the moon were a person, and a woman besides. These lines are from one of his poems; but if a prose writer were describing the state of the sky and should write, "The moon had hidden her face behind a cloud," this would not sound strange to us: it would still be prose. And again, Wordsworth writes—

> "Where lies the land to which yon Ship must go?
> Festively she puts forth in trim array,
> As vigorous as a lark at break of day;
> Is she for tropic suns, or polar snow?"

Here, you see, the *ship* becomes a woman; but there is nothing specially poetical about that, for not only sailors but landsmen have got into the habit of calling a ship *she*, no matter what its name is. So when Cowper, telling of the sinking of the British ship-of-war (yes, *man*-of-war) the *Royal George*, wrote:

> "She sprang no fatal leak,
> She ran upon no rock,"

he spoke as a landsman would ordinarily speak, in spite of the fact that the vessel bore a man's name.

Still, we cannot do much of this personifying or personification, as it is called, in prose, while in poetry there may be any amount of it. In Tennyson you will find these lines—

> "Of old sat Freedom on the heights,
> The thunders breaking at her feet";

while Milton has these—

> "And in thy right hand lead with thee
> The mountain-nymph, sweet Liberty."

In the same poem, Milton had just before described

> "Sport that wrinkled Care derides,
> And Laughter holding both his sides";

and in like manner Coleridge pictures a land

"Where Toil shall call the charmer Health his bride,
And Laughter tickle Plenty's ribless side."

The painters and the sculptors (who are also poets after a fashion) could not get along without personification. There are some famous examples of this in the painting by Guido called "Aurora," and in the statues by Michelangelo called "Twilight and Dawn."

There is no harm in such personification, which is often extended to countries. Thus, one of the patriotic songs of England is "Rule Britannia!" and the first postage-stamp ever made (it was made in England, in 1840) was a picture of Britannia sending out letters to all parts of the earth. We Americans have our patriotic song too: it is "Hail Columbia!"—by which we mean the United States, and if we make a picture of Columbia we always draw a woman. But there is another personification of the United States, and that is "Uncle Sam," or "Brother Jonathan," just as there is another personification of England, and that is "John Bull"; and you will sometimes see drawings of these also. But it is a curious fact that while Columbia and Britannia get along very well together, Uncle Sam and John Bull are always quarrelling. When we feel ourselves just human beings and Christians, members of the great family of mankind, then we let the poets show us Columbia and Britannia working in harmony together to spread the blessings of peace and industry. But when we think of ourselves as Americans, and " patriots," and " the greatest country on earth," and all that, why then it is Uncle Sam who will teach John Bull a lesson, and the talk is all of war and murder and devastation.

Now this kind of personification is mischievous and dangerous, for there is really no such person as John Bull or Uncle Sam. *Englishmen* live in England—not John Bull; and when any one of them comes over here, we treat him well—we are glad to see a native of the country which our forefathers left when they crossed the ocean to settle this continent. But the moment he is gone and we think of John Bull, then we want to fight with our old enemy, and we imagine all the dreadful things he is plotting against our peace and industry. But if we should actually make war on John Bull, he would vanish out of sight, and our guns would destroy English men and women and children who were never our enemies, nor ever wished us any harm. And John Bull would never be able to hit Uncle Sam with his guns, but only you and me, our relatives and friends, and the other inhabitants of this country who do not hate Englishmen.

You would naturally think that if Uncle Sam stands for the United States of America, we could never treat him badly; but in fact people do things to Uncle Sam for which they would be put in prison if they did them to you or me. There used to be a rhyme that

"Uncle Sam is rich enough to give us all a farm,"

and people will cheat Uncle Sam of land, of timber on his land, or of taxes, because "Uncle Sam" is rich enough to bear the loss. But, I repeat, there is no such person as Uncle Sam. You and I are Uncle Sam. All the land he owns, you and I own, and anybody who cuts down and carries off the trees standing on it, is robbing you and me; and if he refuses to pay his taxes, he robs you and me. A thief breaks into the post-office and takes all the stamps and money he finds. Do we forgive him because he is only plundering "Uncle Sam"? No, he has made *us* poorer.

This is how the evil arises: First we take a great number of persons and roll them into one, and call them Uncle Sam, the Government, the State, and then we think we are at liberty to swindle this imaginary person out of everything we can lay our hands on. Just so those who are dishonest or ignorant treat corporations. Corporations are bodies of men and women who put their money together as stockholders for a certain object—as, to carry on a manufacturing business. An employee of the corporation who would not pick the pocket of any one stockholder, will yet (as we often see) rob the corporation if he gets a chance. He looks upon the corporation as a rich and miserly old fellow who can stand being robbed, and then takes from him money that may belong to widows and orphans who have invested their money in the corporation, and who *are* the corporation. This is what comes of turning real people into ghosts—for these personifications are only ghosts, and when was it ever wrong to rob a ghost? There is the corporation known as a College, with its property in buildings and books and works of art. Among its students are boys who have been honestly brought up, but who, from a love of mischief and a desire to be talked about, will smash its windows, carry off its bell, or smear the buildings with paint. They have made a ghost of the College, and they feel no sense of wrong-doing or of shame. These same boys will take down and carry off the street signs in the college town. They have made a ghost of the corporation known as the Town, and so, they say to themselves, we have not been stealing—we have only been joking. The judge does not think so when they are caught by the police and brought before him.

Nothing is easier to make than these ghostly personifications, and they shall be good spirits or bad, as we please. Corporations are usually classed among the bad spirits, and that is why so many of the laws heavily taxing them have been passed. The men who have earned money and saved it are, strange to say, the bad spirit known as Capital, while men who work for a living—or who work with their hands for a living, or who are employed by other people and are not employers themselves—are the good spirit known as Labor. Then we are asked to believe that all that Capital does is wrong and harmful, and all that Labor does is right and beneficent; Labor must make all the laws, and Capital must not make any; you must vote for Labor and against Capital, and so on. But they are both ghosts: "Capital" never earned a dollar in his life, and "Labor" never did a day's work.

There is another ghost called the State, and we are told that if the State only owned all the land, and owned and managed all the railroads and all the telegraphs, everybody would be happier and better off. But there is no such person as the State. The State is, first, all the inhabitants of a country; then it is the Legislature for making the laws; and, finally, it is the officers—Governor, judge, sheriff, policeman, postmaster—for executing the laws and carrying on the public business. It is sometimes convenient to speak of the State as it is of the Government, or Capital and Labor, or Nature, or Art; but the State has no business of its own, no hands of its own, no goodness or badness of its own. It is only a name for you and me trying to live peaceably together, and doing the best we can with the wisdom that we have and the good will one for another.

The Capitol at Washington.

VIII

THE FLAG.

AS we go up and

THE FLAG

AS we go up and down the country nowadays, we notice that almost every schoolhouse has an American flag flying over it or near it while school is in session. Perhaps we are looking for the building and it is hidden from view; but if only we see the flag floating above the trees, we say to ourselves as we walk along, "There must be the school." In this way the flag becomes the *badge* of the school, and saves the trouble of painting or carving the word School on the front of the building, as is often done. When I was a boy and lived in the city, nearly every family had its name—Smith, or Jones, or Robinson—fastened upon the door of the house in which it lived. This kind of sign was called a doorplate; and the flag serves as a doorplate for the schoolhouse. They might have chosen a white flag with the words Public School printed upon it in dark letters, but they chose instead the Stars and Stripes or what we also call the Star-Spangled Banner; and so the flag means not only, "This is a schoolhouse," but a schoolhouse in the United States of America. And it has still another meaning, which is that our native country, the United States, is proud of its schools, and thinks there can be no good government where boys and girls are allowed to grow up in ignorance, without learning the alphabet, to read and to spell and to write, to multiply and subtract, to think and to reason, and to fit themselves to lead honest and useful lives. Who does not love a flag that means all that?

But how do we know from the Stars and Stripes that the schoolhouse is in the United States? Because that is the *national* flag. Nations too, like private citizens, need their badges and doorplates; and so England has one kind of flag, and France another, and Germany another—as many flags as there are peoples and governments the wide world over. This is found very convenient when they have any business with each other, especially in trading on the ocean. The American ship flies the American flag, the Norwegian ship the Norwegian, the Spanish the Spanish, and so on. When they meet at sea, the flag shows just what country the ship belongs to, and what language is spoken on board; also, that the vessel is a peaceful trader and not a pirate.

A pirate vessel, belonging to no country and the enemy of all, used to fly a black flag with a skull and cross-bones figured on it, and this stood for robbery and murder. There is, however, another way in which nations have to do with each other besides buying and selling and exchanging goods in vessels. Sometimes, alas! they go to war with each other, and then the flag shows that on this side is the German army, on that the French, these are American soldiers and those are Mexican; or again, this is a Japanese gunboat, that is an American monitor, that is an Italian torpedo-boat. The same flag, then, has two very different meanings—one of peace and one of war.

We ought to be thankful that our school flag is the flag of peace. There are no guns or swords here, and we are studying not how to kill human beings, but how to make them happy and to put an end to all wars. That was grand when, in 1847, a ship flying the American colors —Red, White, and Blue—brought food to the starving people of Ireland from the kind-hearted people of this country, who had heard of their dreadful suffering. But suppose we had then been at war with Ireland, and had sent our navy over to keep food from coming into the island, and had bombarded the towns along the coast with cannon-balls and set them on fire—all the while the miserable inhabitants dying of hunger by thousands—what sort of a flag would the American flag have been then?

Before the year 1808, our laws permitted American ships to go to the coast of Africa for black slaves. The traders in that country would make war on peaceful villages, set them on fire, kill all who resisted, and drive the rest down to the sea, where the American slave-ships were waiting for them. Then the poor creatures were forced into the hold of the vessel, where they were packed close to each other like herring in a box. Every morning many were found dead from the heat and the foul air, and their bodies were thrown overboard to the sharks that followed the vessel. Those who lived to the end of the voyage—perhaps only half of them—were then made slaves in this country, and had to work without pay, and were sold like cattle, and treated more brutally than any animals. All this was done with the American flag flying from the slave-ships at sea and from the national Capitol at Washington on land; and what could the poor Africans have thought of such a flag? What would *you* have thought of it had you been in their place?

But in 1808, the law having been changed, American citizens were forbidden to engage in this horrid business of the slave trade. What had been right the year before now suddenly became wicked, and the slave trade was treated like piracy—like robbery and murder. The American flag was unchanged: there was the blue field with as many stars in it as there were States; there were the red stripes and the white—but the red color was perhaps not such a bloody red as before. It was as if the flag had been washed, and oh! if the washing had only been thorough and all the blood-stains had been got out of it at that time. But of course there would have been no slave trade if there had been no slavery anywhere, and in 1808 there were a million slaves in this country, who either had been brought from Africa or were the descendants of such as had been.

I once saw one of these slaves who had run away from Virginia, a slave State, to Massachusetts, where slavery was forbidden by law, and where he was now earning his own living. His master had found him in Boston and got him put in jail. You ask, How was that if Massachusetts did not allow slavery on her soil? It was because the Constitution of the United States allowed runaway slaves to be pursued and caught anywhere in the Union, and there was a special Fugitive Slave Law, as it was called, which had just been passed by Congress. The people of

Boston hated that law, and they tried to prevent the slave (whose name was Anthony Burns) from being carried back to slavery. He could not have been carried back if the United States Government had not ordered its soldiers to guard him through the streets crowded with excited people. I saw this poor black man, whose only crime was that he was born black, surrounded by soldiers with loaded guns as they marched to the vessel that was to take him to Virginia. I do not think those soldiers had any flag flying that day, but if they had, it must have been the American flag. Now Anthony Burns was an American, if black; but what did the flag of his country mean for him? It meant turning him from a free man into a slave again. On some Fourth of July he might have heard it praised by white men, by slaveholders, as the Flag of the Free; but he knew, did he not? that this was not true. It did not become true till after a fearful war between the slave and the free States, which broke out in Kansas not long after Anthony Burns was dragged away from Boston, and which ended in Virginia in 1865. Then at last the law forbade the holding of slaves anywhere in the United States.

You will not find much about this in your schoolbooks because people want to forget that the American flag was ever a flag of wickedness and cruelty. But we ought not to forget it, any more than we ought to forget that man was a savage before he became as civilized as he is now. And then, every one ought to know that slaves could be held in slavery only while they were ignorant; and that to keep them ignorant the law made it a crime to teach them the alphabet, to read and to spell and to write, to multiply and subtract, to think and to reason. But if there had been public schools everywhere for white children, it would have been impossible to prevent black children from learning something from the white. So there were almost no public schools in the slave States, even for white people. Now, since slavery was abolished by the war, there are schools all over the United States, and that means that there can never be any more slavery in America, for schools and slavery cannot live together. So when we hoist the flag at the school door, let us remember that it is not the flag of Washington's time, for that stood for a country half ignorant and enslaved; but of Lincoln's, which stands for schools and freemen in all the land.

The Santa Maria.

IX

PATRIOTISM.

TO make an alphabet

PATRIOTISM

TO make an alphabet of famous ships, we should probably begin with Noah's Ark for A. For B we might take the ship *Beagle*, in which. Charles Darwin made his voyage round the world; for C, our American frigate *Constitution*, built in 1797, and perhaps the very oldest vessel afloat. And, thus going on, if we did not find a ship for every letter, we should certainly find more than one ship for some letters. For S, I think we should all want to take in Columbus's ship, the *Santa Maria;* and what should M stand for if not for the *Mayflower*, in which the Pilgrim Fathers sailed across the Atlantic from Holland and England?

One hundred and two of them—men, women and children—were on board of her when they looked for the last time on the English shore; and just as many saw for the first time the low sand-ridge of Cape Cod. True, there had been one death on the long passage, but also one birth;

and this little ocean-born Oceanus Hopkins, what sort of a world was it on which he opened his eyes? He found himself on a floating island, with water all around it and no land in sight. But he was not alone on this island, as Robinson Crusoe was on his. There was a governor or king, known as the captain of the *Mayflower*, whom everybody had to obey. There were his officers—the mates, the boatswain, the ship's cook, the crew. There were his subjects, the passengers: Oceanus Hopkins was one of these, and the youngest. Strange as it may seem, this ship tossing up and down at sea was the babe's country; all the people about him were his fellow-citizens. He could not hear them, sick and weary, wishing that they were back in Old England, or that they were safely landed in America. He knew nothing of either country; he was too young to understand the language spoken about him; the English flag flying from the masthead meant nothing to him.

And now if we could imagine that the *Mayflower* never came to land, but went drifting up and down the ocean, and that Oceanus Hopkins grew up to boyhood on board of her, and began to hear talk of other ships, and now and again to see one on the distant horizon, we might be pretty sure that he would think his native ship the best in the world—the handsomest, and the fastest, and the most comfortable—and his fellow-passengers the finest people in the world. He would, in other words, be very "patriotic"; and the fewer ships he saw, and the more ignorant he was of the kind of people aboard of them, the more patriotic he would be, and the more he would despise foreigners. Nay, if the *Mayflower's* company should some time put into port, and should kidnap the inhabitants on shore and carry off their provisions and their valuable goods, perhaps we should find Oceanus Hopkins hoisting a flag with the inscription, "My country, right or wrong!"

Something like that, indeed, happened about fifty years ago, when we were waging war with Mexico in order to rob her of some of her territory and make it part of the United States. To tell the story properly I must begin a new alphabet of ships—this time not with Noah's Ark, but with the *Arbella*, which sailed ten years after the *Mayflower* from England to Salem in Massachusetts, bringing over a company of Puritans to the newly founded settlement there. A descendant of one of the best and best known of these Puritans was living at the time of our Mexican War, and knew what the war was for, and that the true name for it was land-piracy. The people of the

United States did not all approve of the war, and he might have taken sides with those who opposed it; in fact, he was expected to do so, but when he came to run up his flag, people read on it, "Our country, however bounded!" That meant, "No matter how we enlarge the boundaries of the United States — whether by lying, stealing or killing." You see, this did not differ much from Oceanus Hopkins's motto, "My country, right or wrong!" even if *his* country was a ship.

Suppose some of the Pilgrims on the *Mayflower*, as soon as they had left England, had concluded to give up the idea of settling in America, and to turn pirates, sailing wherever ships were to be met with and captured at sea, or wherever there was a coast to plunder. This is all very foolish to suppose, but we will suppose further that a majority agree to it, while the remainder cry shame upon it, and refuse to have any share in the piracy or in the booty. Should we think it an answer to these honest men to say that they were unpatriotic; or should we think the majority had any right to call themselves the only genuine patriots? No; yet when you come to read the history of the Mexican War, you will find that those who approved of taking by force from Mexico what belonged to her, pretended to be the real American patriots, and called it treason to oppose the war.

It would be very strange if right and wrong were to be decided in this way. The majority of a chance lot of people on board of a ship; the majority of a chance lot of people in a city, in a State, in the United States—these may have some right to govern the rest, but their actions are still to be judged like any other men's. "This war of yours is a wicked war," they are told; and what is their reply? "You are no patriot. The majority are for the war, and are we not all bounded on the north by Canada, on the east by the Atlantic, on the south by the Gulf of Mexico, and on the west by the Pacific Ocean?" "Certainly we are," answers a New Yorker, "but what of that? Manhattan Island, on which I live, is bounded by the Harlem River and the East River and the North River, and will always be so bounded, but it is not always well governed. Just now honest citizens are in the majority and govern the island by means of the police. If the mob should rule it, no man's life or property would be safe. When the mob gets the upper hand of the honest citizens, is it unpatriotic to try to put down the mob? What has the East River to do with that—or the Harlem, or the North River?"

The place where we were born; the spot of

earth, be it large or small, on which our fathers and their fathers lived and died—we cannot help loving that; we are used to it, we know no other either at all or half so well; it is our country. Patriotism begins there, just as charity begins at home. But patriotism does not stop there. The Indians loved this land before we did. Foreigners now come to visit it and admire Niagara Falls, the Great Lakes, the Rocky Mountains, the Yellowstone Park, the Mississippi River, the Yosemite Valley; but that is not patriotism. If, however, they wish that their own country had such beautiful and magnificent scenery, that is patriotism. And if we in turn visit Europe and envy England for its justice, or France for its fine roads, Germany for its learning, Italy for its art, and wish America to be their equal in all these respects—that again is patriotism. To think our country, merely because it is our country, well governed, just, free, civilized, superior to all others, having nothing to learn from any other—that is not patriotism, that is folly.

There are even people—fellow-citizens of ours, fellow-Americans—who not only think it unpatriotic to admire a foreign country, but who would have us hate it as an enemy; and hate it the more, the more it surpasses us, especially if it has learned how to manufacture more cheaply than we do, and wants to sell us some of its cheaper goods. "What," you ask, "must we hate a country that makes living easier and less costly for us?" "Yes," say they, "it is treasonable to buy cheap goods abroad when you can buy dear goods at home." These same people, I remember, a few years ago, said the American flag did not belong to Americans who were willing to let these cheap goods come into the country for the sake of all who were unable to purchase the dearer goods made at home.

If we could not love our father and mother without hating some one else, we could not call that a pure love. Nor is that pure patriotism which cannot love our country without hating England. A great Englishman, Thomas Paine, who came over here and helped us in our Revolution against his own Government, thought himself a good patriot when preventing his country from doing wrong by oppressing the colonies. We too thought him a good patriot, for we accepted his help. He loved the little island where he was born like Oceanus Hopkins in the *Mayflower*, but he hated nobody for being born somewhere else. "Independence," said he, "is my happiness, and I view things as they are, without regard to place or person; my country is the world, and my religion is to do good."

Desiderius Erasmus.

X

EQUALITY OF THE SEXES.

BOYS have been known

EQUALITY OF THE SEXES

BOYS have been known to say, "I'm glad I'm not a girl"; and we might suppose they were thinking of those troublesome skirts which make walking or running, or climbing fences, or playing ball or tennis, or mounting ladders, or even going up and down stairs, less easy for girls than for boys, especially if the skirts are long. But perhaps what they had in mind was the girl's being more confined to the home and going less abroad to see the world, having to share in the household drudgery of cooking and washing, sweeping and dusting and making beds, of nursing the sick, and being themselves, as a rule, not so strong and hearty as their brothers. Perhaps, again, boys have noticed that a girl's education is not expected to be as thorough as theirs; not so many go to college, though the number of girls who do go is increasing every year. Then, when boys come out of school or college, they have to earn a living, and this keeps them busy, whereas a girl who has done with schools and teachers and who does not have to work for a living, often finds the time hang heavy on her hands for want of an occupation.

Still, I think it was not out of pity for girls that the boy was glad he wasn't a girl. He might be ashamed to tell you the real reason, but we can guess it with the help of the story told by Fra Salimbene. This Italian priest, born in Parma, was an infant when the city was shaken by a mighty earthquake in the year 1222. His mother, in great alarm lest the neighboring church should fall on their house, caught up her two little girls, one under each arm, and ran off to the home of her parents, leaving the baby boy in his cradle. As no harm came to him, she could have done no better for him, but Fra Salimbene, when he grew up and heard her tell of this, lost a little of his love for her; "for," he says, "she ought to have been more concerned about me, a man-child, than about the girls." There you have the boy's idea that he is more precious and better worth saving than the girl; in other words, that he is what is called a superior being—not exactly as man is superior to the horse and dog and the other lower animals, but somewhat so.

Now as every boy has a mother, who was once a girl, he cannot set himself above the girls and look down upon them without treating his mother in the same way. If he is superior to *all* women, he must be superior to her; yet it is commonly noticed that boys take after their mother in looks or in mind, as girls take after their father. Great men, too, are in many instances—perhaps oftener than not—found to have had mothers of unusual strength of character. However this may be, the mother has generally far more than the father to do with bringing up the children and forming their character for good or for evil; yet it is only within the past hundred years that people have come to see that if we would have good children, we must have good mothers, and that we cannot take too much pains with the education of our girls. A great Dutch scholar, Erasmus by name, saw this more than three centuries ago, and wrote in favor of women's learning Latin in order that they might be better mothers to their children. People in his time said that it was improper for a woman to learn Latin; that it took away what little brains she had, and made her twice as silly as before. You may read in the Life of Benjamin Franklin written by himself, that, when he was a boy in Boston, he disputed with another boy whether it was proper to make scholars of women, and whether they had wit enough to study. Franklin thought they had, and that it was proper to teach them. Almost everybody thinks so now.

Men do not ask to be told what is manly and proper for the male sex to do, but they have always wished to say what was womanly and proper for the female sex to do; for is not man the superior being? The Greeks and Romans would not let women act on the stage at their theatres, and if you should go to a Chinese theatre to-day you would see the female parts all played by men. In our theatres, men and women act together, and it would be hard to tell which act best. I can remember when it was thought strange and indecent for a woman to speak in public, especially if there were men in the audience; now, nobody objects to her doing so, and the men who go to listen to her think they may learn something from her, even if she is a woman. They were willing enough to learn their a b c from her in the schools, their writing and arithmetic and geography; but they used to think that was all she had to do with the schools. Now, they begin to give her a place on the school committee, and even to let her vote on school matters, thinking that mothers ought to take an interest in the education of their children. In my boyhood days this would have been considered very unwomanly, and in all but a few parts of the United States it is still thought improper for women to take the same interest in politics that men do, and to vote at town and State elections. So they cannot help to make the laws they must obey, or choose the men who are to carry on the government, for this is considered none of their business.

Man, you see, still wants to feel himself superior to woman in something, and able to get along without her advice or aid. She has eyes, like him, and he can no longer deny her the right to see, even if she turns astronomer and gazes at the stars through her telescope. She has limbs, and he has always been ready to have her do her full share of lifting and carrying heavy burdens; she may walk and run as much as her skirts will allow her, and she may even shorten her dress a little and wear trousers in order to ride the bicycle. She has a voice, and may sing or preach or lecture. She has brains, and may read and think, study Latin and Greek, write books, paint pictures, practise law and medicine and architecture. She may now, for all he cares, do almost everything a man does except vote and be voted for, though there is nothing difficult about that. Government is only a kind of housekeeping, and it is surely woman's business to keep house. While she continues to wear long dresses that trail upon the pavement, is she not interested in having clean streets, for example? Once, in a German city, I saw a gang of women sweeping the streets in the early morning. Americans would be apt to think that unwomanly, or at any rate would rather see it done by men; but what is there unwomanly in dropping a little piece of paper in the ballot-box to choose men (or women) who will have the streets cleaned honestly and without waste?

We must not blame the boy who says, "I'm glad I'm not a girl." Nobody asked him to be anything but a boy, and he is only repeating what hundreds of boys have said, from Fra Salimbene (who thought one boy worth at least two girls) down. All we ask of him is to let girls be girls. Whatever he would like to do for himself, let them be suffered to do as they may be able. When Sancho Panza was made governor of an island, a physician stood beside him at table with a long rod, to let him eat only what he thought fit for him. And by this means Sancho was all but starved, for first a dish of fruit on which he had begun was suddenly touched with the rod and taken from him, because it was too moist, and then a dish of meat because it was too hot with spice; neither must he taste hare's-meat nor partridge, neither veal nor stew. "Some hundred of little hollow wafers and some pretty slice or two of quince marmalade" was all that the physician allowed this hearty eater. In like fashion man (on the pretence that he is a superior being) has treated woman. Only now he is beginning to see that in cramping her he is cramping himself also; that, as Tennyson says in his poem, "The Princess"—

"The woman's cause is man's; they rise or sink
Together, dwarfed or godlike, bond or free. . . .
If she be small, slight-natured, miserable,
How shall men grow?"

St. Mark's Square.

XI

SANITY.

THERE are twenty-four

SANITY

THERE are twenty-four hours in each day, and if ever you should go to Venice in Italy, you might see on St. Mark's Square a clock with twenty-four hours on its face. That is because the Italians used to tell time from one o'clock to twenty-four o'clock. *Our* clock-faces have only twelve hours on them; and when the clock has struck twelve for midnight or for midday, we expect it, at the end of another hour, to strike only one—not thirteen or fourteen. Still, most of us have heard a clock strike fourteen times or more—yes, strike as if it would never stop. "It must be crazy," we say. We take it to the clockmaker, and he says it is out of order.

A man too gets out of order, for his body, like a clock, is a machine; and if the parts do not all work together as they were meant to do, something will surely go wrong with him. The lungs and the heart and the stomach and the liver and the kidneys and the intestines are to the body what the wheels and pinions, the weights and the pendulum and the springs, are to the clock. When any one of those parts of the body which we call organs cannot, for any reason, do the task it was set to do, then there is trouble all around: we do not feel comfortable, we suffer pain, we fall sick; perhaps we die. Sometimes the trouble is in the brain and makes a man act queerly. People say of him, " He has a screw loose," just as a machine may have; or they say his mind is unbalanced, as if it were a pair of scales—or unhinged, as if it were a door.

Such a man was Don Quixote, the hero of a famous Spanish story. He was a mad knight who rode up and down the country in search of adventures. One day he discovered a lot of windmills in a field, and thought they were monstrous giants. He spurred his horse at one and thrust his lance into the sail, which was turning round in the wind at a great rate. His lance was broken, and he and his horse were lifted off the ground and tumbled over upon each other. The foolish Don still thought he had been fighting giants, who had been turned into windmills. Some time afterwards, on a dusty plain, he came upon two flocks of sheep, which he took for two armies marching against each other. Into one of these he rode furiously, lancing the poor sheep right and left as if they were his enemies, until the shepherds nearly killed him with stones from their slings. And still he thought he had been attacking men, not sheep. He saw things not as they really were, but as he imagined them.

Don Quixote had with him a squire or serving-man, named Sancho Panza, who saw things truly, and tried to keep his master from these crazy actions. "I pray you understand," said Sancho, "that those which appear there are no giants, but windmills; and that which seems in them to be arms, are their sails, that, swung about by the wind, do also make the mill go." And so with the sheep. "Dost thou not hear," asked the Don, " the horses neigh, the trumpets sound, and the noise of the drums?" "I hear nothing else," answered Sancho, "but the great bleating of many sheep." Sancho was what we call sane, and Don Quixote was insane, or out of his senses, or not in his right mind.

Very sad is it not to be in one's right mind. Our minds are not all alike. Some men are born with great minds and become inventors, like Edison, or poets, like Shakspere, or musicians, like Wagner, or soldiers, like Napoleon, or statesmen, like Lincoln, Gladstone and Bismarck, or naturalists, like Darwin; and their names are known all over the world. But most of us have either common minds, or little minds by which we just manage to get along from day to day. When we wish to speak of the difference in minds, we say that one man has more brains than another. Now Don Quixote certainly had more brains than Sancho Panza. He was a learned man with a library, and was all the time reading his books, while Sancho hardly knew his a b c. Yet Sancho's mind was perfectly sound. It would not hold as much as the Don's mind—it was not so large a cup; but the Don's cup was cracked, and we all know that when we go to the spring, a whole cup is better to drink out of, even if it is small, than a big cup with a leak in it.

Now what should we think of a man who had to draw his water in a bucket from a well, yet took a gimlet and bored holes in the bottom of the bucket? This would be very much like a man who, having a sound mind, should set to work to make it unsound. Such a man is the drunkard, who takes liquor into his stomach until he does not know where he is or what he is doing. He tries to walk, and does so as if he were on board a ship, with the deck pitching up and down under his feet. He reels and staggers along, and thinks the earth is rising up in front of him, as it might do in an earthquake. He no longer sees things as they are; he is as insane as

Don Quixote. And oh what dreadful things men do when they have made themselves insane with drink! It is not the worst that they may fall down and hurt or kill *themselves;* for sometimes they get furious, and then they may savagely beat or kill their wives or their children, just as the Don slaughtered the innocent sheep whom he mistook for soldiers. When the drunkard's madness is over, he remembers nothing of what has happened. Drink has stolen away his brains for a time; and the more he drinks, the more he is robbed of his brains, till at last he has no mind left.

There is an old saying that to have a sound mind, you must keep the body sound. We can do this in two ways: by taking exercise at work or in play, or again by avoiding everything which harms the body and its organs. No one needs to be told not to let his arms or his legs or his head be cut off or smashed if he can help it: we all have sense enough for that even if we are sometimes careless. But to eat too much or too fast, to eat food which disagrees with us, to swallow it before we have fairly chewed it, to injure the teeth by drinking water too cold, or tea or coffee too hot—these are some of the things we all need to remember and to be cautioned about. When the stomach is out of order from indigestion, caused by improper feeding, then the mind is affected: we lose our cheerful spirits, we take (as is said) a gloomy view of things, and expect troubles of our own imagining. A windmill looks like a giant; a flock of sheep like an army; a molehill like a mountain. We cannot see things as they are. Our friends notice the change in us, and say, "You are not yourself any more." But not to be yourself is to be, partly at least, out of your mind, to be unsound and insane.

So we must govern our appetites if we wish to be ourselves and not to be insane even for an hour. We must also govern our passions. See how an angry person storms and rages, and what dangerous and wicked things he will do, and how he repents them when his passion is over. An angry boy throws a stone at another and puts his eye out. "I did not mean to," he cries. Of course not; he would have been a savage if he had meant to. He was beside himself with rage, and had no control any more over his will and his senses. Anger is a short madness. So is fear. Shakspere says: "The thief doth fear each bush an officer." That is, with his guilty conscience, he mistakes in the dark a bush for a man, and that man a policeman. He cannot see things as they are. Again, in times of great danger, as in case of fire or of shipwreck, people are apt from fright to lose their presence of mind: they either do nothing, or do the most foolish things —carry the feather beds carefully down stairs and throw the looking-glasses out of the window. They are in a fever of excitement, and in fevers we often become delirious, we dream out loud, our minds wander and our wits are lost. Not so with those who keep cool and do not get excited and feverish; they see just how great the danger is, and just what can be done to escape it. They are not too frightened to act at all, neither do they act as if they were crazy; they do not run down like a clock, nor do they strike fourteen times at the noon hour of twelve.

The Brooklyn Bridge.

XII

THE INSATIABLE MIND.

A MAN'S mind is not

THE INSATIABLE MIND

A MAN'S mind is not exactly like a Paris omnibus, on which the driver puts up the sign "Full" when it will hold no more passengers. We should laugh at any one who went about with such a sign on his forehead: "Full—no more ideas can get in here." A *school*, to be sure, is something like a railway-train, which all the passengers have to leave when the journey's end is reached: "All out for Boston—for New York—for Chicago! All out for the Grammar School, for the High School, for College! Make room for a new set of passengers and a new set of scholars." But however far the mind is carried along in education by teachers, it cannot be said to have reached its journey's end. It has still something to learn, and, if there are no teachers to be had, it can teach itself.

We often speak of furnishing the mind, and of the furniture of the mind, as if we were talking about a house. But what is a furnished house?

It is not the archway built of twigs by the Australian bower-bird, for example, into which he brings a heap of land-shells and sea-shells, bones and bright-colored feathers. It is not a robbers' cave, either, like that of the Forty Thieves in the story-book called the "Arabian Nights," where Ali Baba found all sorts of provisions, together with bales of silk, carpets, and piles of gold and silver. A furnished house must have rooms in it, and each room must have its proper furniture —books for the library, pictures for the parlor, china for the dining-room, a cook-stove for the kitchen, beds for the sleeping-rooms, and so on. Of course, the better the house, the better will be the books, the more costly the pictures and the table-service, the more comfortable the beds. And even in the same house, if the owner grows richer he will put away his old furniture and buy better; and this is very much like the mind, which, if it continues to grow, will all the time be changing its tastes, will no longer be content with what once pleased it, and will seek for something higher and more beautiful for its own adornment.

Now what school does for us is to show us where to go for the mind's furniture, how to choose good furniture and not bad, and what may be done with it after we have got it. You might think, because all the pupils in one class are taught the same amount of arithmetic and geography and spelling and writing, that what school is for is just to cram the mind with knowledge, as if the mind were a bowl or a bushel basket. We can fill a bowl with soup or with milk or with peas or with pudding—the bowl does not care what it holds; but give the mind the multiplication-table, and what wonderful things it will make out of it! There is the architect, whose glorious temple or palace or church is in ten thousand parts all carefully measured and fitted to each other—so many feet and inches broad, long and deep. There is the builder of the Brooklyn suspension bridge, who calculates exactly how solid the granite towers must be to sustain the wire cables, what load of cars and foot-passengers the cables will bear, and also what pressure from the wind blowing over the East River. There is the astronomer, who discovers how far off the sun is, and tells to a minute when it will be eclipsed and in what parts of the globe the eclipse will be visible. You see, the mind not only receives knowledge, but makes use of it to get more.

There is a wildflower, called the pitcher-plant, which has a pouch or sac covered inside with a sticky fluid that insects are fond of; and so arranged with prickly hairs that when the insects get down they cannot crawl back, and are consequently drowned in the fluid and become food for the plant. The plant digests them just as the stomach digests the meat we give it; and in a similar manner the mind digests the knowledge that it gets from being taught in the first place, and then from thinking for itself. The stomach does no thinking, and the pitcher-plant does none; they are only living machines which work as long as they are fed. Nor can they get food for themselves as the mind gets it. Give the stomach its three meals a day and it is satisfied; the mind is never satisfied. It may be starved as the stomach may be starved, but it will take all the training that school can give it, and still will desire to learn and to find out more than it has been taught.

This is a dreadful thought for boys and girls who suppose they have got through with their minds when they have done with school. How delightful are the holidays and the long vacations when there is no school! And now to be told that the mind takes no holidays! It is enough to make children almost wish they had no mind, or not more than the horse's, the dog's, or the cow's. They sympathize with the youngster in that funny poem by Mary Lamb:

> "I saw a boy with eager eye
> Open a book upon a stall,
> And read as he'd devour it all;
> Which when the stall-man did espy,

Soon to the boy I heard him call,
'You, sir, you never buy a book,
Therefore in one you shall not look.'
The boy pass'd slowly on, and with a sigh
He wish'd he never had been taught to read;
Then of the old churl's book he should have had no need."

True it is that if we once begin to learn the alphabet, there is no telling where the love of learning may carry us. Few of us will ever after that be content with minds like those of the lower animals; and there is no end to the ways in which the mind that is curious and not easily satisfied can occupy itself and be happy. One of the things that school does for us is to show us how many such ways there are to choose from. To look over a plain we must rise above it, and the higher we rise the wider will be the prospect. The primary school is a little mound; the grammar school and high school are the foot-hills; college and the university are the mountain ranges with vast views in all directions. *Now* we can take our pick of what lies below; and as on a map we see our country divided off into States, and the States into counties, and the counties into towns, so, in looking over the vast field of knowledge, we see it cut up into squares and sections of all sizes to suit every taste. Instead of States and counties we call them *-ologies*. Thus, Geology is the science of the globe on which we live; Zoölogy is the science of animal life on the globe; Anthropology is the special science of mankind; Ethnology is the science of the several races of men; Ornithology is the science of birds—Entomology, of insects—Ichthyology, of fishes; Meteorology is the science of the weather. Then we have, besides, Botany for the study of trees—Astronomy, of stars—Chemistry, of substances. I could never repeat the whole list.

We cannot all reach the top of what is sometimes called the ladder of learning; but for that very reason we ought to lose no time in climbing as high as we can. Nobody was ever so learned that he could not wish he had been better taught. Many persons with little or no education have been successful in life and become famous; yet these "self-made men," as we call them, often regret their want of education. The child thinks of the long days at his desk when he might be playing out of doors; he sees the vacation coming to an end; he counts up the years he must still spend over his books, and he gives a sigh of weariness. The man, on the other hand, looks back with a sigh and recalls how many hours he wasted in school, how little attention he paid to the recitation, what trouble his mischief caused the teacher, and how it prevented the studious from fixing their minds on their lessons. But it is now too late. There is a French proverb which says, "If Youth but knew; if Age but could."

The Matterhorn.

XIII

ATTAINMENT.

THERE comes to my

ATTAINMENT

THERE comes to my mind a story of a village high up among the Alps. Night was fast setting in before a threatening storm; the torrent roared; an avalanche of snow was ready to fall on whoever should try to cross the mountain by the narrow pass. A youth is seen climbing the road. The kind-hearted villagers warn him of his danger, but he will not stay and take shelter with them. He carries a banner on which they read, but do not understand, the motto, *Excelsior*—that is, *Higher, still higher! Upward, still upward!* He passes on into the dark and is lost to sight. The next morning, at daybreak, his dead body is found in the snow, his hand yet grasping the banner.

> "There, in the twilight cold and gray,
> Lifeless, but beautiful, he lay,
> And from the sky, serene and far,
> A voice fell, like a falling star,
>   Excelsior!"

You all know this story from Longfellow's poem, of which I have quoted the last stanza. But, now that you think of it, was it not odd that anybody should want to write a poem on such a subject? If the youth had actually got to the mountain-top in spite of the tempest and the ice and the falling limbs of the withered fir trees—why, that would have been something to brag about and to write about. Or if he had got there one hour, sixteen minutes and twenty-eight seconds sooner than any other climber had done, and so had "beaten the record"—as the newspapers say of a fast-sailing ship or a fast-trotting horse—why, then again we might throw up our caps over that, and shout hurrah, and make rhymes to celebrate it. On the contrary, the poor fellow never reached the top, and his climb was a failure; and why should poets bother themselves about failures?

We shall ask this question frequently if we notice how much noble poetry has been written about the weak and suffering and unsuccessful, and particularly about those who lost their lives in some vain endeavor. Take the soldiers who fall in battle—and in a losing battle—and in a war that is a losing war, like the Revolution of 1848, when the Italians strove to free their country from its Austrian rulers in order that it might govern itself. Take the martyrs for conscience' sake, like the Waldenses of Piedmont in Upper Italy, who in 1655 let themselves be driven from their homes and massacred rather than give up their religion and turn Catholic at the command of their cruel prince; or like the Quakers of Massachusetts, who, about the same time, let themselves be sold out of the country, and even be hung, rather than give up their religion at the command of their cruel Puritan rulers. You will find poems worth reading and remembering about all these unfortunates; and there is a famous sonnet of Wordsworth's on Toussaint L'Ouverture. Toussaint had been a black slave in San Domingo, one of the West India Islands. The French Republic emancipated him and all his fellow-slaves in 1794, and he became Governor of the island. In 1802, Napoleon sent an army to make them all slaves again; and, though he did not succeed, he seized Toussaint and carried him off to France, and put him in a damp dungeon in a mountain fortress, where he quickly died, as Napoleon meant he should. But Wordsworth's fourteen lines on Toussaint, written while he was still in his dungeon, and beginning—

"Toussaint, the most unhappy man of men!"

are worth more than all the poetry ever written about Napoleon by his admirers and flatterers.

Now how shall we explain this praise of people

who fail? If we look closely we shall find that it is not the failure, but the *trying*, that is honored by the poets; and then the trying, the endeavor, or it may be simple endurance and suffering, must be for some good and lofty purpose. The burglar who fails to break into your house, for instance, is not a subject for poetry although he may have worked hard all night; he is a subject for arrest and trial and punishment. The judge and the poet agree in telling him,

"Not failure, but low aim, is crime."

On the other hand, to the Italian patriots of 1848, resisting Austrian oppression, but defeated, the poet says:

"Ah! not for idle hatred, not
For honor, fame, nor self-applause,
But for the glory of the cause
You did what will not be forgot."

Then he goes on to comfort them with the thought that whether they succeeded or failed was a matter of chance or fortune, and that it was better to have fought and lost than never to have fought at all.

It is so with every one of us. What would happen if nurses and doctors refused to attend the sick because cures are uncertain? or if parents paid no attention to bringing up their children in good habits and principles because some children, well brought up, go astray and turn out bad? The doctor says, "I must do my duty." The parent says, "I must do mine." Success is a matter of chance, but we can and must do our duty, and, when we have done that, we are satisfied with ourselves, or, in other words, our conscience is satisfied. If the doctor had *neglected* the patient who died, or if the parent had neglected the boy who became a drunkard or a gambler, that would have been a different thing. The *faithful* nurse, the faithful mother, have succeeded if they have only done their best.

How is it in school? Some of the scholars were born bright and quick-witted, eager to learn and apt to learn; others learn painfully and slowly. Some have parents who were well taught and who help them along in their studies; others have parents without any education, and who think going to school is a waste of time. The teacher soon finds out who are her best scholars and who are the dullest; but she also finds out which try to learn (though they may be among the dullest), and which are lazy and inattentive (though they may be among the brightest). She knows that it is not success to do less than you can, even if you stand at the head of the class; and not failure to do all that you can, even if you stand near the foot. If she had the Excelsior banner to give as a reward, very likely it would go to a scholar who often learned his lesson in tears. That would be a prize for character—for will and determination and effort in spite of all discouragement.

This, after all, is the only real success. The head scholar in the primary school is not sure of being the head scholar in the grammar school, still less in the high school, and still less in college. The boy who has four cents in his pocket is richer than his playfellows who have none, but he will feel himself poor beside the boy who has a quarter of a dollar—and he may meet that boy at any time. To outrun a one-legged man is, for a man with two legs, a sort of success, but how about winning a race with men who are as sound of limb as he is? There is a proverb which says that in the city of the blind the one-eyed man is king. Put this one-eyed man in a city of the two-eyed, and what was his advantage among the blind becomes a disadvantage. In short, it is easy to be better than some one else, but not to be best of all.

What is best in all the world to-day will not always remain the best. Man is constantly growing wiser and wiser, and is not satisfied with what contented his ancestors. The turnpike and the stage-coach were once looked upon as great successes—that is, as great improvements on the old modes of travelling in mud and mire; but what are they now to the railroad and the steam and electric cars? and what will these be to the flying-machine which any of you may live to see? One success calls for another and a grander success, which we name our ideal; and as soon as we overtake it a fresh ideal starts up, and we have to go in pursuit of that. Then everything behind us seems a failure, though each failure has helped us on the road to success—or rather on the road to perfection—and this road has no end. Never mind, we must still press forward. The road is steep and slippery with ice—no matter: *Excelsior!* Upward, still upward! One of us falls in the snow: it is Toussaint, murdered by Napoleon, but his country is now a land of freemen; or it is the Italian patriot of 1848, shot dead at Peschiera, but his country too at last is free—the Austrians have left it forever. *Excelsior!*

> "Each one must do his best, and all endure,
> And all endeavor, hoping but not sure."

Mainz.

XIV

SUPERSTITION.

NOBODY ought to leave

SUPERSTITION

NOBODY ought to leave school without learning something about the art of printing. This art has now been practised by the people of Europe and the rest of the civilized world for four centuries and a half. We are not quite certain where it was invented, but in all probability this took place in the valley of the Rhine. Among the famous cities along the banks of that river is one called Mainz by the Germans, but which on the map you will probably find spelt Mayence, after the French fashion. In that city is a public square, known as Gutenberg Square, in which stands a statue of John Gutenberg, the man who first discovered how to print with movable types.

Now what are types? Thousands upon thousands of people read printed books and newspapers all their lives without ever having visited a printing-office, or really knowing or being curious to know what types are and how they are set. Types are little pieces of lead, about an inch long, with a letter on the upper end of each one; and when you look at a page of your reader or speller or geography, every letter of every word you see was picked by hand out of boxes containing an assortment of all the letters of the alphabet—the *a*'s by themselves, the *b*'s by themselves, and so on. Not only that, but every punctuation-mark —every comma, period, dash, apostrophe, semicolon, interrogation-point, and the rest—was likewise picked out of a box. And finally, wherever you see a white space separating two words, there a type shorter than the others, and having no letter-face on it, had to be picked out and used to keep the words from running together. The letters are thus first set in words, the words are next divided off into lines, the lines are divided off into pages, and then everything is ready for the pressman, who rolls a thick ink over the types, lays a sheet of paper on them, and presses the paper down on them with his machine.

Such is the art of printing, and if you will count the number of letters and punctuation-marks and spaces in a page, you will learn how many times the compositor who set the types had to lift his hand to bring them all together into their right places. Sometimes he makes mistakes: he leaves out a letter, he picks up the wrong letter, he turns a letter upside down. If any one not used to setting type were to try his hand at it, he would make a great many more mistakes; and if he picked up the types at random—that is, without knowing or caring which was the *a* box or the *b* box, and so on—when you came to print what he had set, you would find it nonsense: it could not be read. We must, then, set type with *intelligence*—that is, we must know how to spell and what we want the types to say, for types do not set themselves.

Supposing the words to have been correctly spelt and put in order by the compositor, whether a book shall then be good sense or nonsense (yes, whether it shall be wise or foolish, useful or harmful) depends upon the maker—that is, the author or writer. When a child learns how to talk, we do not expect him therefore to speak always sweetly and politely and cleanly; in fact, we take the greatest pains to keep him from hearing rude and vulgar and profane words, lest he should repeat them even if he does not understand what they mean. So, knowing how to read will not keep him from reading bad books unless he is warned against them and made to loathe them. And if, on growing up, he is able to write a book himself, no one can tell in advance what sort of a book it will be. It is not the best speller who writes the best books; nor is it the best scholar.

The education that we get at school does not of itself make us sensible, wise, good and just, kindly, merciful, helpful. Very important it is to learn how to write; and yet if we use that knowledge to imitate some one else's handwriting, in order to steal money or for any other base purpose, we commit a crime, the crime of forgery. Just so it is a fine thing to be skilful with tools, but it is a crime to use that skill as a burglar uses it, to break into a house or into a safe that he may rob it. To be good citizens it is not enough to learn the alphabet: our jails hold plenty of men who have had an excellent education as well as men who have had none at all. Boys who have been to school and to college together, pursuing the same studies under the same teachers— do we expect them to be equally upright and virtuous as men? No; that would be contrary to all our experience. Men who have been taught that two and two make four, that Rome is the capital of Italy and is situated on the River Tiber, and that Constantinople was taken by the Turks in 1453, about the time when Gutenberg was printing his first book, will all agree as to these facts. But ask them whether war is a good thing or a bad thing, whether nations (like men) should love their neighbors as themselves, whether public office should be held for the public benefit or for private gain, whether a man's right to vote should depend upon his color or a woman's upon her sex, and what different answers they will give, and how differently they will behave!

School, we can only say, makes us less ignorant, and saves us from a great many foolish opinions and actions which proceed from ignorance. What we call superstition—that is, beliefs or fears for which no good reason can be given—is caused by ignorance, and we find it everywhere. Thus, our American Indians did not like to have white men come among them to paint their portraits as Mr. George Catlin did many years ago. One chief died soon after his portrait was painted, and his friends and relations believed that the painting was the cause of his death. But then, there are in some parts of Scotland people who, though not savages, object even now, when photographs are so common, to having their likenesses taken, for the same reason as the Indians, or a similar reason; and among them must be some who can read their Bibles and other books. Superstition about "lucky" and "unlucky" still exists in spite of school and teacher. Many well-educated persons will not sit down at a table of thirteen; the month of May is avoided by those who marry; Friday is thought to be an unlucky day for a ship to sail from port; the breaking of a looking-glass is considered a sign of coming misfortune; the spilling of salt between two persons sitting at table means that they will quarrel, and so on.

Our Puritan forefathers, though not a few of them were educated men, brought over with them a quantity of superstitions, like those I have just named, which are yet to be found among our ignorant population. Increase Mather was a clergyman, a graduate of Harvard College and for a time its President, but, like most of the men of his day in New England, he believed in witches, or bad spirits in the shape of men and women, who did harm to people merely by looking at them with an evil eye, or by wishing them ill, or by making them sick without touching them in any way. One of his most popular sermons, preached about two hundred years ago, was on Comets or Blazing Stars, which he called "Heaven's alarm to the world." Nowadays no sight is less alarming or more welcome than that of a beautiful comet in the sky, but Increase Mather (and the New England men generally) looked upon it as a fearful sight, and a sign of great calamities at hand. When the smallpox broke out in Boston, or a destructive fire raged, or when the land was shaken by an earthquake, these old New Englanders thought God was angry with them for their sins.

We must not laugh at them. They had not been setting type and making books as long as we have been. They knew very little about nature, about the human body, about medicine; numberless things which are clear to us were mysterious and awful to them. Why is that poor girl pining away if some witch is not casting a spell upon her? Why have wars followed the appearance of comets unless comets are the cause of war? This was the way in which our fathers reasoned in their ignorance. Why did that chief die soon after Mr. Catlin painted him if portraits do not make people die? So reasoned our North American Indians in their ignorance; and, though they had no schools and only a kind of picture-writing, they reasoned as well as our forefathers who founded Harvard College and established the first printing-office in the United States. They reasoned as well as people do nowadays about matters which they have not studied and do not understand—for instance, about money and about the laws of trade. We must remember that a man learned in some things may be quite ignorant in others, and that the half-educated man is apt to think he knows everything. All the foolish as well as all the wicked laws ever made in this country (and we have had a shameful number of both) have been passed by men who had had some sort of schooling, part of whom knew how types were set, and a part might have seen in Mainz the statue of Gutenberg.

The Wolf of the Capitol.

XV

PLASTICITY.

SHAKSPERE, in one

PLASTICITY

SHAKSPERE, in one of his plays, imagines the mighty Greek conqueror, Alexander, to have died and been buried and turned to dust, and this dust to have mingled with the common earth about it, and then to have been used by some one to stop a bung-hole. And passing from Alexander to the greatest of Roman generals, Shakspere next supposes that

> "Imperious Cæsar, dead, and turned to clay,
> Might stop a hole to keep the wind away."

A Persian poet, Omar, had a similar fancy—that the earthy remains of the dead, instead of plugging a beer-barrel or patching a wall, might chance to be used to make pots and other vessels for holding liquids. "For," he says—

> "For I remember stopping by the way
> To watch a Potter thumping his wet Clay:
> And with its all-obliterated Tongue
> It murmured—'Gently, Brother, gently, pray!'"

Now making clay into shapes of earthenware, or moulding it as a sculptor does into images, we call a plastic art; and clay, wax, butter and other like substances capable of being moulded and modelled, we call plastic substances. Snow is one of these, as we prove when we make snowballs and snow forts or a snow man out of it; and ice too is plastic, for it can bend without breaking under its own weight, and in the shape of glaciers it will flow down a mountainside like a river, though very, very slowly. Even the rocky globe on which we live is plastic, for it is not perfectly round, but is a little flatter than it should be at the poles; and this comes from its revolving on its axis and not being entirely stiff and rigid. In fact, it is best to think of everything as plastic in some degree.

However, when we have divided substances into those which are easily moulded (like butter, snow, wet sand, clay, wax, and melted glass) and those which are not (as, the granite out of which the architect makes the blocks and columns for his building, or the marble out of which the sculptor carves his statue), we still must bring them all together again under one class, namely, that of dead or inert substances. These are nothing like so plastic as living substances, or those which form the animal and the vegetable kingdoms. This class of living and growing things we also call *organic;* the other class, inorganic. Grass, a flower, a tree, a worm, an insect, a fish, a bird, a horse, a man, are organic; rocks and earth, iron and copper, water, the air, are inorganic. You might find on the beach a pebble resembling an egg, but if you placed it in a museum it would remain unchanged for ages. On the other hand, let a real egg be hatched in the barnyard, and see how the plastic yolk and white of the egg have shaped themselves into a little feathered chick, and then watch the chick swell and grow into a hen, or into proud chanticleer with his gorgeous tail-feathers, his ruddy comb and gills, his voice that wakes us all in the early morning. Or plant a chestnut in the moist, warm earth, and watch the meat or flesh of the nut burst the shell and sprout up into what will one day be a spreading tree. Cut off this tree at its base, and see how many shoots will push forth from the stump, each in turn becoming a tall tree growing out of the ruins of the parent tree. Some of the lower animals, if they lose a limb, can grow another in its place. The salamander, which is like a lizard in appearance, can do this if it has parted with its tail or a leg.

Man is not as plastic as a salamander, but he can do a great deal to alter the shape of his body.

We cannot make ourselves taller at pleasure, though by proper exercise we can make ourselves more erect. According to the kind and amount of our food and drink, we can keep lean or grow stout. Practice in running or in climbing hills will surely broaden and deepen the chest; much walking or riding a bicycle will enlarge the calves of our legs; the use of Indian clubs in the gymnasium will fill out the muscles of our arms. In fact, any part of the body which is much used suffers some change of form or texture to fit it to its use. How tender is the sole of a child's foot when his mother first lets him run without shoes and stockings in the warm weather; and how soon it thickens so that he does not mind the pebbles on which he treads!

What are called the domestic animals, such as dogs, cats, horses, cattle, swine, poultry, have been bred by man for thousands of years, to suit his needs or his fancy; and they have been as plastic in his hands as if they had been clay or putty. Think of the enormous variety of dogs alone, and consider how the bulldog's face has been kept fierce as a watchdog's should be, yet by way of a joke we have put this face, like a mask, on a ladies' pugdog, which looks so fierce and is so timid. Yes, our animal-breeders are able not only to mould a race-horse or a draughthorse, a milk-cow or a butter-cow, but they can give the disposition and temper which they desire the animal to have.

The plastic *mind:* if there were no such thing as that, we should have no need of schools. There are stories of children that have been suckled by wolves (as Romulus and Remus were said to have been) and have afterwards run wild with them, snarling and snapping at men. It might prove a difficult task to take a wolf's whelp and train it to behave like its civilized cousin the dog—to be affectionate, to follow at your heels, to guard and respect your property, not to touch food not meant for him. But there would be some hope of changing the wolf-boy into a civilized boy, by clothing him and petting him and showing him how to behave in the company of others, how to eat with knife and fork at table, and to prefer cooked food to raw meat; putting him at school and teaching him his letters, how to study and to pay attention and to remember, to think and to reason. By and bye, after much patience, we should find the wolf-boy's mind moulded quite as really as dead Cæsar's clay.

Our American Indians are not wolves, they are our fellow-men; but in some of their ways they are as fierce and cruel as wolves. We take their children and bring them from the Far West to schools in the East, in Pennsylvania and Virginia, and we find it easy to teach them manners and morals, books and trades, and start them well on the road to civilization. When they leave Carlisle or Hampton, they are far more intelligent and refined than were our British forefathers when Julius Cæsar landed in England and seized that country with his Roman army; and this was less than two thousand years ago. The Romans were at that time the masters of the known world. Now the English and the English-speaking Americans together are the most powerful peoples on the face of the globe.

It might seem a fine thing to have a plastic mind; but because the mind can be moulded, we must not suppose it will always be moulded right. Give any one a lump of clay and he can scoop some kind of a pot out of it, or make an image somewhat like the human figure. But these will be far from having the beauty of the pottery and the statuary of the Greeks, for example. What is worse, the potter or the sculptor may not *intend* to produce something noble or beautiful, but only what is hideous and vile. It would be bad enough if our minds were trained by others to admire what is evil and despise the good, but we ought not of our own choice to shape them so. The clay can do nothing to be shapely except as it is thumped by the potter and turned upon his wheel. It cannot look up to some lovely statue, such as the Venus of Melos, and strive to be like that. The mind, on the contrary, can pick out its models from among the wise and the good of past ages, and strive to grow up in their likeness. If it feels for them an affection—that is, a leaning or a drawing towards them, an inclination, a movement—the mind is already plastic, self-shaping. It can besides (such is the miracle of human character) make even the blows of fortune or of malice lend an added beauty to its form.

Louis-Jacques Mandé Daguerre.

XVI

CONSEQUENCES.

NEAR the very beginning

CONSEQUENCES

NEAR the very beginning of the "Arabian Nights' Entertainments" you will find the story of the Merchant and the Jinn. Merchants we all know, but which of us has ever seen a jinn? A jinn, in fact, is generally *not* seen, for the Arabs, and other Mohammedan peoples in the East, gave this name to spirits who (they pretended) were usually invisible, yet who could appear in divers shapes of man or beast.

Our merchant, then, was abroad on a journey for business, and stopped on a hot day to rest and cool himself in the shade of a wayside grove. And as it was lunch-time, he made a meal of the dates which he carried with him, and threw away the stones as he ate. He then washed his hands, said his prayers, and was still on his knees when a monstrous jinn suddenly appeared, sword in hand, threatening his life. "Rise up," said the jinn, "that I may kill thee, as thou hast killed my son." "*I* kill your son?" cried the poor merchant; "I did not know him and never saw him." "Did you not," answered the jinn, "take dates out of your portmanteau, and, as you ate them, throw the stones about on both sides?" "I cannot deny it," said the merchant. "At that time," said the jinn, "my son was passing by, and you threw one of the stones in his eye, which killed him; therefore I must kill you." Nor would the jinn listen to the merchant asking for mercy, as having killed the son unknowingly and innocently.

I cannot stop now to tell you whether the jinn actually killed the merchant or not. The story as it stands will serve well enough to fix our minds on the consequences of our actions. Some of these consequences are easy to foresee, but some are invisible, and often a well-meant and innocent act may have very disastrous consequences. Give a little baby bright-colored beads or marbles to play with, and he may swallow them and choke to death; give him a closed penknife, and he may open the blades and cut himself. Parents have to think of these things all the time. So when, out of pity, we give money to the poor, we may be doing them harm instead of benefiting them; for what if they should use the money to buy liquor? In towns and cities during the winter, when there is little work and much poverty, sometimes soup-kitchens are opened to feed the destitute. Then it is found that the poor who are not destitute come for soup like the others; and as the news of the kitchens gets abroad, the worthless poor, who never work, but live by begging and stealing, flock into the place to be fed for nothing. The town is then worse off than before, for it has more paupers, and it is encouraging the lazy and wandering habits of those we call tramps.

On the other hand, there are plenty of examples of the happy consequences of right action far surpassing what we could have expected. Benjamin Franklin, before he left Boston to go to live in Philadelphia, came upon a book of "Essays to Do Good," by Cotton Mather, a clergyman of Boston. The book was torn, "but the remainder," says Franklin, "gave me such a turn of thinking as to have an influence on my conduct through life, for I have always set a greater value on the character of a *doer of good* than on any other kind of reputation; and if I have been a useful citizen, the public owes the advantage of it to that book." Now Franklin himself wrote a book, his Autobiography, which has been translated into a great many languages, and which, wherever it has been read, has helped to make men better. Nobody reads Cotton Mather's book any longer, but Franklin's Autobiography is still read, and the good it has done and is doing is part of the consequences of Cotton Mather's Essays.

Franklin, you will remember, drew down lightning from a thunder-cloud by means of a kite, and thus proved that lightning was the same as the newly discovered electricity. Long afterwards, another American, Morse, invented the electric telegraph, but he could hardly have imagined that the same wire over which the electricity travelled, would presently be used to *talk* over, as we do with the telephone, between places a thousand miles apart, to drive our cars for us and our machinery, light our houses and perhaps some day heat them.

What we call photography was invented about sixty years ago by a Frenchman named Daguerre. He took portraits and other pictures on a copper plate, and these were called daguerreotypes. Little did he dream that this would by and bye enable us to make pictures not merely of the outside of a man but of the inside; that the very bones of the body could be photographed in a dark room and with the clothes on, and that the surgeon could thus learn if a bone was broken, or where a bullet or a needle had lodged in the flesh. It was a German named Roentgen who taught us this wonderful kind of photography, but his discovery was a consequence of Daguerre's.

About the time the daguerreotype began to be perfected, an American, Charles Goodyear, succeeded in treating india-rubber so that it could be manufactured into all sorts of articles. No doubt he foresaw a great many of these uses, but he could not have imagined that his invention had anything to do with road-making. Now, however, we have bicycles with rubber tires, and for riding on them with pleasure we need smooth roads, and therefore such roads are being expressly made all over the country. This is a kindness to horses as well as to bicycle-riders, so that Goodyear was a benefactor to animals without knowing it. He was also a benefactor to women, for they now ride the bicycle and find their health improved by exercise, which they did not use to take before—and if we have healthy women we shall have healthy children. Not only that. A few years ago it would have been thought unwomanly to ride in public on a bicycle, but now the girls begin early to ride with their brothers, and wives ride with their husbands, and nobody thinks any more about it. So Goodyear's invention had for one of its unexpected consequences a change in the bodily habits of women, and in men's opinion of what it is proper for women to do. And even that is not all. Men and women are seen riding on bicycles on Sunday, and yet it used to be thought sinful to seek pleasure or recreation on Sunday. Goodyear's invention, then, is helping to change our ideas about Sunday.

We live in a world in which, whatever we do, we must bear the consequences, be they good or bad. How much we ought to be blamed for them if bad, will depend on whether we can say "I did not think" or "I did not know." The boy who threw his orange peel on the sidewalk says, "I did not *think* that some passer-by might slip on it and break his leg." The answer is, "That is no excuse. You ought to have thought." The merchant protested to the jinn, "I did not *know* that your son was passing when I threw the date-stone in his eye." The jinn would not treat this as a good excuse, though the merchant was really not to blame, for how could he see an invisible spirit? The jinn was not trying to find some one to blame for the death of his son, but some one to punish as the *cause* of it. Nature is a sort of jinn to us. She punishes us for the consequences of our ignorance just as surely and just as severely as for the consequences of our intentional wrong-doing. She has no patience with us while we are learning, and wo be to us if, having learnt, we are careless and neglectful—if, having discovered that smallpox can be prevented by vaccination, we do not get vaccinated; if, having found that typhoid fever comes from foul drinking-water, we let the drainage from the barnyard flow into the well.

Those who take no thought of the consequences of their actions, we call foolish, rash, reckless, imprudent, improvident, or, it may be, wicked. These names, however, have been applied, and misapplied, in all ages and countries, to men who knew very well what harm might happen to themselves if they simply did their duty to their fellow-men. This duty might lead them to resist a tyrant or an evil law from which their land was suffering; to speak out when every one else was too cowardly to open his mouth; to oppose the mob or to oppose the Legislature. The consequences to themselves of their action they did not mind, and were ready to bear as martyrs if need be; the consequences to others —to family, neighbors, countrymen—of their *in*action, they could not bear. They remembered the old saying: "This ought ye to have done, and not to leave the other undone."

Gibraltar.

XVII

CONTEMPT.

IN Mr. Emerson's fable,

CONTEMPT

IN Mr. Emerson's fable, the Mountain spoke very disrespectfully to the Squirrel, who answered him with spirit. "If I cannot carry forests on my back," said the tiny creature, "neither can you crack a nut." Some such reply the monkeys who live on the sides of Gibraltar, in the southern part of Spain, might make to that mountain if it despised them; and as for man (whom some think but a higher form of monkey), small and insignificant as he seems beside the great rock, he could, if you gave him time enough, blow it to pieces. When Gulliver fell asleep in the land of the Lilliputians (who were, as he says, little folk hardly taller than his fingers), and woke to find himself tied to the ground, he thought if he once got up he should make short work with them. He fancied himself a match for the greatest army they could bring against him; but he soon discovered that they had him in their power. Afterwards, as he pretends, he visited

Brobdingnag, a country whose inhabitants were as tall as steeples—say, sixty or seventy feet high. Among such giants he was as much a pigmy as a Lilliputian was to him, and they looked upon him as little better than an insect, a poor timid thing, and laughed at the fine stories he told about what his people could do in their own country.

Nothing is more common than to judge people according to their size, and to think slightingly of those who are small or undersized. But when we come to read the lives of the men who have distinguished themselves in the history of the world, we perceive that some were indeed larger than others, but that if we were to range them in a row, the greatest men would not all be the tallest and stand at the head of the row. Suppose we took the most distinguished captains and warriors; we could not possibly place Napoleon at the foot, little man though he was. And if we were asked whether this Frenchman or the Roman Cæsar or the Greek Alexander was the greatest general, we should be laughed at if we began by getting out our yard-measure to see which overtopped the others.

Often as we may form a wrong opinion of men according to their stature, we are quite as likely to be deceived by their looks. We sometimes say, by way of a joke, that a person is too ugly to live. That was not the reason why the Greeks put Socrates to death, though he was, in fact, as homely as he was good—and he was one of the best of men. Abraham Lincoln was another very plain and awkward man, and if you had merely looked at him, you would never have picked him out to be President of the United States. He was about as tall as Washington, but could not compare with him in beauty or dignity of person. We now, however, often speak of them together as two of the fathers and saviours of their country.

In the matter of looks, we are influenced very much by what we are accustomed to, both in features and in dress, and that is why in all countries strangers are stared at, and frequently annoyed and abused, by the ignorant and ill-bred. The Chinaman's odd jacket and shoes, his pigtail and his almond-shaped eyes—even the food he eats—make our mob treat him with contempt. The Chinese at home, however, are a very remarkable people; they invented gunpowder and the art of printing without any help from Europe; they have their fine temples and statues; their leading merchants and statesmen compare with any in the world; no people is more industrious. If we despise them for their superstitions, who knows that they do not despise us for ours?

Then there is the matter of color. The reason why the white races plume themselves on being white, is probably because the uncivilized races of mankind are all dark-skinned, and some of them have permitted themselves to be made slaves by the white. They have all, nevertheless, done things which we can but admire, and the monuments of the ancient Egyptians and Hindus are among the most marvellous works of man. We cannot trust ourselves to decide that white is a better color than black, yellow or brown. It may be so, but our opinion would probably be different if we were black, yellow or brown. Mr. Darwin, when among the South Sea Islanders, who go nearly naked, noticed that a white man bathing by the side of a Tahitian was like celery bleached by the gardener, compared with a fine dark-green plant growing in the open fields. He said it required little habit to make a dark skin more pleasing and natural to the eye of a European than his own color.

Though we read in the Psalms, "Blessed is the man that sitteth not in the seat of the scornful," the tall scorn the short; the handsome the homely; the white the dark. The rich also feel themselves much superior to the poor. There is no reason for this. In all countries, though in some more easily than in others, the poor become rich without changing their natures; or they make the great discoveries which contribute so much to the happiness of mankind; or they rise to be the rulers of those who were born rich and were perhaps descended from kings. In our Southern United States, before the Civil War put an end to slavery, there were four classes—the whites who owned slaves or hired slaves; the whites who could not afford to own or to hire them; the slaves themselves; and the free blacks. The richest and proudest of all these were the slave-owners, mostly planters, and they despised the "poor whites," as they were called, who had to work with their own hands to make a scanty living, and who were generally a very ignorant and shiftless folk. One of these "poor whites" in Kentucky, who could not write, married in 1806 a woman of the same class who could read and write a little. Like all their class, they had, as we say, no social position whatever; the rich whites would not associate with them, and even the negroes thought them of no account. They could not hold on to the land they tried to farm, and at last they resolved to do, what so many "poor whites" had done before them—cross the Ohio River and settle in one of the new Northern States where slavery was forbidden. They took with them their little boy born in 1809.

Nobody missed them when they went. Had they stayed in Kentucky, in all probability we should never have heard of them. The child would have grown up as ignorant and shiftless as his parents, to be despised like them and kept in poverty. Yet this child was no other than Abraham Lincoln; and in the terrible war which the slave-owners made against the Union because he was elected President, he it was who abolished slavery, and made it respectable and honorable for a man, whether black or white, to work anywhere at the South with his own hands. This is what is meant in the Jewish Scriptures when we read that "God chose the foolish things of the world that he might put to shame the things that are wise; and God chose the weak things of the world that he might put to shame the things that are strong; and the base things of the world, and the things that are despised, did God choose."

We often speak of the flower of a family or of a people, meaning the pick of it—the favorite or most promising child, or the most enlightened class of society. When the Lincolns crossed over into Indiana, they did not go as the flower of Kentucky; they did not belong to society at all. The flower of Kentucky thought itself well rid of them, and the people of Indiana could not have been very glad to receive them. Our Puritan forefathers did not permit strangers to come among them who seemed likely to be a burden and charge upon the town because they could not support themselves. Nobody, judging the Kentucky boy Lincoln by his looks and his circumstances, could have seen any promise of greatness in him, and he was in fact an exception to the rule that the poor and untaught do not blossom out and acquire honor and power and a world-wide fame. Encouraging as his example is, we must not therefore think it better to begin poor and untaught. Flowers we must still try to raise, but we can do so without despising the lowly. In our human garden,

> "some are but weeds,
> And yet from them a secret good proceeds."

The Parthenon.

XVIII

VICISSITUDE.

ALL over our Northern

VICISSITUDE

ALL over our Northern valleys and hillsides we notice huge rounded stones, either partly buried in the earth or resting upon it, which we call boulders. They are different in kind from the rock of the neighborhood, and to find anything like them we often have to go many miles further north. They are fragments of mountains, and have been brought where they are either by fields of ice in motion, called glaciers, which once covered all this country to a great depth, or by the floods caused by the melting of so much ice. The rock on which the Pilgrim Fathers landed at Plymouth was one of these boulders, dropped on the sandy shore of Massachusetts Bay, and hence a pilgrim itself from its old mountain home. The glaciers are now gone, but the mountains are still being lowered. The wind and the rain, the snow and the frost, the sun, fire, lightning, earthquakes, all work together to wear down what the poets call the everlasting hills, but which are so far from being everlasting that more mountains have perhaps disappeared than are now to be seen—at least on some portions of the surface of the globe. In fact, if they had been made of ice instead of rock, they could not more surely have wasted away than they have done.

But if this happens to the Alps, the Andes, or the Rocky Mountains—if they are slowly crumbling away and rolling down into the plain—it is no wonder that anything which man builds, whether of wood, of iron or of stone, is certain to decay and fall to the ground if left to itself. The best-built house is all the time getting out of repair: roofs will leak, shingles will rot and fall out, mortar will crack, bricks loosen, chimneys blow down, hinges rust, and doors and blinds get unhinged, window-glass break, paint peel off. If the owner is not constantly guarding against these things, his house will "run down," as we say, and, sooner or later, if wholly neglected, it will tumble flat. Everybody has seen such buildings going to ruin, and all over the world are to be found the remains of once solid and costly stone structures which are now no better off than our deserted wooden farm-houses or barns.

Then, too, not only has man the elements to fight with—that is, sun and wind and rain and frost, lightning and earthquake—but he is a great destroyer himself. For instance, he alone of all the animals knows how to make fire and to use it; and what with his matches and his lighted pipes and cigars, his candles, his oil and gas and electric lighting, his wood fires and coal fires, his Fourth of July fireworks, he is forever burning up his houses. The oversetting of a lamp may burn up a whole city, as was nearly the case in Chicago in 1871. Man, too, first of all the animals, invented gunpowder and other explosives, and you may read how in 1807 at Leyden, a Dutch city on the River Rhine, once the home of the Pilgrim Fathers, a ship having seventy kegs of powder on board blew up, and caused the destruction of more than eight hundred houses. And this same gunpowder men use in war to destroy each other and whatever comes in their way, whether it be walls and armed forts, or public and private buildings. There was that beautiful marble temple at Athens, built by the old Greeks and called the Parthenon. Nothing on the face of the earth was so fine, or better deserved to be saved and protected. Two hundred years ago, in 1687, the Turks were the masters in Greece and were attacked in Athens by the Venetians, who bombarded the city. The Turks had stored some of their powder in the Parthenon, and the powder, being struck by a bomb-shell, exploded, and wrecked the temple, doing more harm to it in one instant than the elements had done in two thousand years; the roof and the middle portion with the long lines of columns on both sides being torn out, never to be built again.

Like the mountains, and like the work of his own hands, man himself is continually being pulled down, and has ever to be contending against disease, accident, violence and poverty, and, if he be rich and powerful, against the envy and jealousy of others. You remember how Robinson Crusoe's father advised him to keep to the middle state in life, saying that "kings have frequently lamented the miserable consequences of being born to great things, and wish they had been placed in the middle of the two extremes, between the mean and the great," having neither poverty nor riches. Perhaps, too, you have heard the story of Crœsus and Solon. Crœsus was a king of Lydia, a country in what is now known as Asia Minor. Solon was a wise man of Athens who made laws for that city. Crœsus had conquered many nations and had become very rich when Solon paid him a visit, so he took great pains to show off his wealth to him. This done, he asked Solon who was the happiest man he had met in his travels. As Crœsus had everything he desired, he expected Solon to name him as the happiest man; but Solon, who was no flatterer, named two or three humble citizens who had spent useful lives and died gloriously, saying that until a man was dead he might be called *fortunate*, but not happy—"for the Deity, having shown a glimpse of happiness to many, has afterwards utterly overthrown them." Crœsus, who had meant to make a handsome gift to Solon, now let him go without any, thinking him a very ignorant man "because he disregarded present prosperity, and bade men look to the end of everything."

Some time after this, Crœsus, not satisfied with the power he already had, made war on the Persians, whose king was Cyrus. But now at last he was defeated and taken prisoner, and Cyrus (in those barbarous times) resolved to burn him alive. In fact, the pile of wood to which Crœsus was fastened had already been kindled when he cried out with a groan, "Oh Solon, Solon, Solon!" This excited the curiosity of Cyrus, who asked him what he meant, and on learning that Crœsus remembered Solon's saying that no one could be called happy while still living, he ordered the fire to be put out and spared Crœsus his life, but took away his kingdom from him, together with all his riches.

This was twenty-five hundred years ago, but

we do not need to go so far back for examples of the truth of Solon's saying. At the beginning of the year 1812, Napoleon Bonaparte was the greatest monarch in Europe; his empire embraced nearly the whole Continent, and it seemed as if his armies could conquer and overrun any country not yet submitting to him. Up to this time he had been fortunate, and as his happiness consisted in extending his power, no doubt he really thought himself happy. Solon would rather have thought happy some of the men who died in resisting Napoleon, and would have said to him, "Look to the end." Napoleon, however, looked only to the present. As Crœsus, at the height of his power, made war on the Persians, so Napoleon, at the height of his, determined to make war on the Russians. He did enter their country and defeat their army, but he could not stay there in the bitter winter season, and had to retreat to France, losing the greater part of his army in the terrible cold. All the other nations which he had conquered now rose against him, and he ended his life as a prisoner on a little speck of an island in the South Atlantic Ocean.

We speak of this as the downfall of Napoleon Bonaparte, as if a huge image had been overthrown. Such a downfall was that described by the poet Shelley when he tells of meeting

> "a traveller from an antique land
> Who said: Two vast and trunkless legs of stone
> Stand in the desert. Near them, on the sand,
> Half sunk, a shattered visage lies."

Shattered though it is, the frowning and haughty face shows that the man it represented must have been some great ruler accustomed to be feared and obeyed. What more did the traveller observe about this statue?

> "And on the pedestal these words appear:
> *My name is Ozymandias, King of Kings:*
> *Look on my works, ye Mighty, and despair!*
> Nothing beside remains. Round the decay
> Of that colossal wreck, boundless and bare
> The lone and level sands stretch far away."

Yes, Robinson Crusoe's father was right: we need not envy those above us. The higher their station, the more terrible their fall. And Solon too was right: we cannot be sure that our good fortune will last as long as we live. Is any one proud and boastful of his birth, his family, his titles, his treasure, his land, his palace, his castle, his power?—let him heed the voice of the prophet crying: "Who art thou, O great Mountain? Before Zerubbabel thou shalt become a plain!"

Buddha Images at Tokyo.

XIX

DEATH.

THE people of Japan

DEATH

THE people of Japan are passionately fond of flowers. A great many of their holidays are fixed by the blossoming of trees and shrubs. These festivals are known as flower-viewings, when everybody is expected to be out of doors enjoying the rich colors of the landscape. Thus, at a time of year when we are celebrating Washington's birthday, perhaps with the thermometer at zero and snow over all the ground, the Japanese have their plum-viewing; the plum blossom being the first to put forth after the snow is gone. This happens commonly in February. In April is the cherry-viewing; in May it is the peonies which cause the schools to close, in August the lotus, in November the chrysanthemum—and these are only a part.

Blossoms do not last forever in Japan any more than in any other country, and no doubt the people are sorry to see them drop and fade away, especially when the fruit is worthless (as in the case of the Japanese plum tree). Still, the Japanese do not have fast-days or mourning-days when the flower-viewing is over, but go cheerfully about their work till the next bloom-time comes. They know that

"Leaves have their time to fall,
And flowers to wither at the north wind's breath."

They know that the fruit lasts but a little longer than the blossom out of which it grew, and that the tree itself must sooner or later decay and crumble into dust.

Suppose, however, that, in the midst of the plum-viewing, one Japanese should say to another: "I wonder you can be so happy at the sight of these blossoms, which have but a short time to live, and whose falling petals will soon be making the ground pink. For my part, I feel like having a good cry." That would sound doleful and melancholy enough, and we should think that such a man could never be cheerful, or do anything but cry, since every living thing has but a certain time to exist—some insects only a day, some men a hundred years, some trees five hundred or a thousand years; all at last coming to an end. We must make up our minds to that once for all; if not, good-bye to happiness. Most of us, indeed, actually do try to enjoy life as we go along, and do not sorrow because the world is full of change, beauty loses its charm, strength turns to weakness, and the number of living beings is vastly smaller than the number of the dead.

Still, you will find that most people think it more natural for flowers and trees, flies and birds and four-footed animals to die than for man. We all, of course, admit that men are born and die just as worms are born and die; that human beings perish of famine in India by the hundred thousand just as fish perish by the hundred thousand when a volcano vomits its hot ashes into the sea; that herdsmen and cattle alike are frozen to death in great snow-storms on our Western plains; that when a ship sinks at sea, the passengers on board and the rats must go down together. But if death from accidents like these, or in consequence of sickness, happen to one of our own relatives or friends—and especially if it happen suddenly and unexpectedly, and to the young—then it seems to us most unnatural, we grieve as if nothing of the kind had ever been heard of before, we put on mourning, we refuse to be comforted. Storms seem as natural as fair weather, even though they blow down my barn; night seems as natural as day, even if I lose my way and fall into a ditch; but why should death take from me my mother, my baby brother, my wife, my child, my dearest friend?

We cannot think long about this matter before it becomes plain that death is just as natural as birth and life, and that no one of us can escape the fate of all living things. We ought, therefore, to feel no *surprise* at the loss of one who is near and dear to us. Nor ought we to grieve too much; any more than we should rejoice too much in the birth of a child who may become either strong and happy, or weak, sickly and miserable —either good and useful, or vicious and mischievous to his fellow-men—and who in any case cannot live always.

> " Every night and every morn
> Some to misery are born;
> Every morn and every night
> Some are born to sweet delight,
> Some are born to sweet delight,
> Some are born to endless night.
> Joy and woe are woven fine,
> A clothing for the soul divine;
> Under every grief and pine
> Runs a joy with silken twine.
> It is right it should be so:
> Man was made for joy and woe;
> And when this we rightly know,
> Safely through the world we go."

And how often, as we go through the world, we are reminded that there are many things worse than death, which is, after all, only a sleep and a forgetting. When we look at our jails and our poorhouses, our asylums for drunkards and for the insane, do we not feel like wishing that the inmates were all dead—that they had all died rather than come to so much wretchedness and shame? I once knew an unfortunate man who lay for years upon his back, unable to move a limb. "Had I been a dog," he said, "they would have shot me long ago"; and it is true that when a horse, for example, breaks a leg or is otherwise badly wounded, men kill him to put him out of pain. We cannot treat *men* so, however much they beg us to end their sufferings quickly—as wounded soldiers sometimes beg on the battlefield. But when death comes to them, we are glad for their sakes. We are glad, too, when very old people die if they have ceased to take any pleasure in life, having no longer any strength in their limbs, no appetite for food, no eyesight, no hearing; and being left solitary and alone by the loss of friends and relations. Death is a mercy to them also, and with good reason we carve on their tombstones "Here *rests* the body."

We sometimes speak of untimely deaths—that

is, of deaths which happen before a man has become so old that he might naturally be expected to die. Some men, as I have said, live a hundred years or more—seldom much more; but most of us at seventy begin to think of making ready to quit this world, and, if we feel death approaching, do not complain of it as being early or out of season. But there is another sense in which death appears to us untimely, and that is when a useful life is cut off, be the person young or old.

> "Long have I lasted in this world, 'tis true,
> But yet those years that I have *lived*, but few.
> Who by his gray hairs doth his lustres tell,
> Lives not those years, but he that lives them well.
> One man has reached his sixty years, but he
> Of all those threescore has not lived half three;
> He *lives* who lives to virtue; men who cast
> Their ends for pleasure, do not live, but last."

We ought really, then, not to be so much troubled about death as about living. Are our days well spent? Are we active, cheerful, helpful? Do we try to be unselfish and mindful of others in everything that we do, both great and small? Are we tender and generous and loving? Are we honest and truthful? Are we religious in school as in church—in our business as in church—in public office as in church? Then we do truly live, and when death overtakes us, no matter at what age, we shall not ask for more time like the old peasant in the fable, who prayed for death, but repented and would fain have been spared when his prayer was answered. Others may grieve to part with us and may call our going untimely; but we ourselves, having done what we could in the years allowed us, and not knowing what the years to come may bring us in loss of health or fortune or character, are able to look on death without alarm and with a kindly eye, even in the very midst of the flower-viewing.

The Pyramids of Egypt.

XX

HEREDITY.

ONE of the oldest

HEREDITY

ONE of the oldest inhabited countries in the world is Egypt, the land of the Pyramids; and a great deal of what we know about it in ancient times has been learned from the contents of its tombs. The Pyramids themselves were tombs, built to hold the dead bodies of kings; the commoner tombs were sunk in pits or cut out of the solid rock, and in these have been found not only embalmed bodies or mummies, but many articles belonging to them when alive, such as a battle-axe, a necklace, a handglass, a comb, a lamp, a writing-tablet or slate. And since children died in Egypt as well as elsewhere, sometimes the explorers of these tombs come upon a doll which had been buried with the little one.

Yes, for thousands of years, among the Egyptians and among all nations, parents have been fond of their children, and children have been fond of their dolls, which they have carried in their arms, hugged and kissed, nursed, washed, dressed and undressed, and put to bed with a lullaby, just as if real children. I have even heard of *naughty* dolls which had to be punished —of dolls which had the measles and had to have the doctor; and I have known doll-parents to neglect their infants so far as to let them lose arms, legs or heads by rough handling. When children grow older, they have to think about themselves—how they shall be taught, and how they shall earn a living; and the dolls are put aside. That is right, but it would be a pity for the doll-parents to forget that in time they will become real parents of real children like themselves.

There are a great many proverbs about the resemblance of children to their parents. "Like father, like son," is one of these; and how often one sees father and son walk alike, putting their feet down in the same way, and having the same swing to their bodies. Or they may both be left-handed together, or lose their hair early, so that we say baldness "runs in the family." A tendency to consumption or to insanity may run in the family, and in such cases persons sometimes refuse to marry lest their children, too, become insane or consumptive. And truly it would seem a cruel thing to hand down to our children diseases born in ourselves and likely to be born in them.

Whether we thus hand down blue eyes or red hair or hooked noses or white skins is of no consequence, nor can we help it if we would. The Emperors of Austria belonging to the Hapsburg family have not, with all their power, been able to prevent a very ugly lip from being a mark of family likeness from one generation to another. But what is an ugly lip to an ugly disposition, and who would not much rather have a homely face than a sour temper? I remember a good lady who was certainly one of the homeliest I ever knew. She was cross-eyed, and her large, irregular, projecting teeth quite spoilt her mouth; and how much not merely beauty, but just agreeable looks, depend on eyes and mouth! This lady, however, had an excellent mind, which she cultivated by reading and study, and she was very fond of conversation and of sharing her thoughts with others. Moreover, she had a warm and kindly heart, and was full of good deeds, and the moment she began to talk, all this shone out in her face, and you forgot her crooked sight and unshapely mouth, and saw only her beautiful expression—so intelligent that you wanted to learn of her, so humane and friendly that you could not help loving her.

When Indian children are brought East to be taught civilized ways—to dress like white people, to read and write, to sew and to cook, and to use tools—generally, if not always, a photograph is taken of the new-comer; and then, after the boy or girl has been a year or two at the school, another picture is taken, and you would hardly believe that they represented the same person. The heavy, dull, stupid, timid face has been changed—not in the shape of the features, but in the expression, which is now full of life and intelligence. You will see the same change in any school of white or black children, and it shows that if we improve our minds we improve our looks. All that we need is the curiosity and the will to learn, and an eager use of every opportunity to increase our knowledge. Then it will be strange indeed if what we take into our minds does not come out in our faces.

We sometimes hear of a person's having a doll-face, and this means a face with no more character than a rag-baby's, which has sawdust in place of brains. Other faces tell of a lazy disposition, disliking work; others, of a weak will that cannot say yes or no, that puts off doing the thing that ought to be done *now;* others, of selfishness and meanness; others, of a low cunning. But, on the other hand, who does not know the brave and manly boy by his looks, or the bright boy, the active, the prompt, the resolute boy, the generous boy—and all that? And if we are to hand it down to our children, shall it be a doll-face or a character-face; and if not a doll-face, then shall it be good character or bad?

We cannot begin too early to think about this. If we wish our children to have healthy bodies, we must not abuse our own; we must be well and strong ourselves, live as much as we can in the fresh air, be active and busy, eat wholesome food, avoid bad habits of smoking and drinking, get all the sleep we need and at regular hours, take good care of our eyes, keep the pores of the skin open by bathing and exercise. Doing this we may be certain—not that our children will be as sound and vigorous as ourselves; no, only certain that we have done our best for them, and that they cannot blame us for any weakness or defect with which they were born, and which might have been spared them if we had not been thinking of ourselves alone.

So of bodily habits. If we sit and walk erect, instead of lounging or slouching, if we rise early, dress quickly, act promptly, the chances are that our children will likewise be smart and active and punctual, and at least that they will more easily be taught to be so. For while some habits are born in children, others are taught them, and others still they get by imitation of people about them, especially of their parents. Just so is it with character and behavior; and if we grow up without speaking the truth and without being honest, and let our selfishness, our appetites and our passions go without check or denial, then, first, we may expect our children to be born deceitful and thievish, stingy and greedy and intemperate. *First*, I say—and that would be bad enough; but, second, we shall be unable to teach right conduct because our own example is the other way. What can the drunkard father do to keep his son from drinking?

A little more than seventeen hundred years ago, lived Marcus Aurelius Antoninus, one of the best of the Roman Emperors, and ruler not only of Italy but of many countries, called provinces, including Egypt. In a religious book which he wrote in Latin, but which has been translated into many languages and can be read in English at any public library, he tells of his learning by the example of his grandfather not to give way to anger, and by his father's example to be modest and manly. "As for my mother," he says, "she taught me to be a man of principle, to be generous and open-handed, to do evil to nobody, nor even to think of such a thing. By

ERRATUM.

Page 198, line 9 from bottom. For *Latin* read Greek.

her, too, I was brought up in a plain, inexpensive way of living, very different from the luxury of the rich."

This mother was not trying to bring up an Emperor, but just a good man, like his father and grandfather; and Marcus Aurelius really took more pleasure in thinking how to make mankind better, and how to make life noble and worth living, than he did in governing the Roman Empire. His religious book he valued more than any victory in battle. It has become his monument. He went to Egypt with his army, but he did not envy the dead kings *their* monuments, the Pyramids, which indeed can excite our wonder only at the labor and the cost of building them. They are, after all, but a kind of stone mummy-case. They hand down nothing except the name of the mummy inside of them, while the "Thoughts of Marcus Aurelius," as we call his book, though originally written on tablets of perishable wax, or on frail leaves made from the Egyptian papyrus plant, have handed down to this day the lessons of life and character which came to him from his mother and other ancestors.

Happy is the child of such ancestors, but just as happy may any one of us be whose daily thought is how to fit himself to be an ancestor; what to do and what not to do in order to make our children bless us for bringing them into the world—what faults to overcome, what virtues to practise, how to strengthen our bodies and broaden our minds. Not to think of or care for those who come after us may suit a doll; but then, *we* do not live in a toy-shop.

THE END

INDEX

Alexander (356–323 B. C.), greatest Greek general, 143, 164.
Ali Baba and the Forty Thieves, 114.
Alps of Switzerland, Europe's highest mountains, 33; wearing away, 174; view of the Matterhorn, 121; crossing in a storm, 123.
Andes, chief mountain range of South America, 174.
Antwerp, in French-Belgian *Anvers*, 53.
Arabian Nights: story of the Forty Thieves, 114; of the Merchant and the Jinn, 153.
Arbella, John Winthrop's ship (1630), 85.
Asia Minor, a Mediterranean country, 176.
Athens, the capital of Greece, 175; home of Solon, 176.
Attainment, PARABLE XIII., 123.
Australia, home of the bower-bird, 114.
Austria, puts down the Italian Revolution, 124; hereditary lip of her emperors, 195.

Beagle, Charles Darwin's ship, 83.
Bismarck, Otto von (born 1815), a German statesman, 105.
Books, not to be soiled in school, 24, 39; pains taken to make a beautiful page, 24.
Boston, birthplace of Franklin, 95; lets Anthony Burns go back to slavery, 78.
Bower-bird, Australian, 114.
Britannia, a poetic name for England or Great Britain, 65.
Britons, barbarians, 148; conquered by Romans, 60.

Brobdingnag, a country of giants visited by Gulliver, 164.
Brooklyn Bridge, spanning the East River, 115; view of it, 111.
Burns, Anthony (1830–1862), a black American: carried back into slavery, 78.
Cæsar, Julius (100–44 B. C.), Roman general and ruler, 143, 164; lands in England, 55 B. C., 148.
Cape Cod, Massachusetts, first land touched by Pilgrim Fathers, 83.
Capital and **Labor**, 69.
Carlisle, Pennsylvania, Indian school, 148.
Catlin, George (1796–1872), American painter of Indians, 137, 139.
Chicago, great fire of 1871, 175.
Chile, copper-bearing country, 59.
Chinese, invent printing and gunpowder, 165.
Cholera mobs in Paris, 46.
Clocks, with face of twenty-four hours, 103.
Coleridge, Samuel Taylor (1772–1834), English poet, 64; poem quoted, 65.
Cologne, in German *Köln*, 53.
Columbia, a poetic name for the United States, 65.
Columbus, Christopher (1435–1506), Italian navigator: discovers America, 6, in the *Santa Maria*, 83.
Comets, regarded by the superstitious as a sign of calamity, 138.
Consequences, PARABLE XVI., 153; consequences of ignorance and of wilfulness the same, 158.
Constantinople, taken by the Turks, 136.
Constitution, American war-vessel, 83.
Constitution of the United States, the pro-slavery compromises (1787), 56.
Contempt, PARABLE XVII., 163.
Copper, in the United States and in Chile, 59.
Corporations, 67, 69.

INDEX

Cowper, William (1731–1800), English poet: poems quoted, 48, 64.
Crœsus (reigned 560–546 B. C.), a rich king of Lydia, 176; defeated by Cyrus, 177.
Crusoe, Robinson, his father's good advice, 176, 179; alone on a desert island, 84; sees a savage footprint, 25.
Cyrus (died 529 B. C.), king of the Persians, 177.

Daguerre, Louis-Jacques Mandé (1789–1851), French inventor of photography, 156; portrait, 151.
Darwin, Charles (1809–1882), an English naturalist, 105; sails round the world in the *Beagle* (1831–1836), 83; opinion of dark skins and white, 166.
Death, PARABLE XIX., 183; death common, natural and universal, 186; a mercy to the suffering and helpless, 187.
Declaration of Independence, American (July 4, 1776), 56.
Dolls, ancient Egyptian, 193.
Drunkenness, is insanity, 106.

Earthquake, in Parma (1222), 94; earthquakes regarded as signs of God's displeasure, 138.
East River, boundary of Manhattan Island, 87; spanned by the suspension bridge connecting Brooklyn with New York, 115; view of the river, 111.
Edison, Thomas Alva (born 1847), an American inventor, 105.
Egypt, a very old country, 193; wonderful architecture, 166; contents of tombs, 193; Pyramids, 193; later a Roman province, 198, 199.
Emerson, Ralph Waldo (1803–1882), American poet: poem quoted, 8; fable of the Mountain and the Squirrel, 163; portrait, 1.
England, barbarous early inhabitants, 148; country seized by Romans, 55 B. C., 148; called Britannia, 65; personified as John Bull, 65; quitted by Pilgrim Fathers, 83, and Puritans, 85; makes first postage-stamp, 65; laws against defacing

nature with advertisements, 27; its courts of justice, 88; English and Americans most powerful of peoples, 148.

Equality of the Sexes, PARABLE X., 93.

Erasmus, Desiderius (1467–1536), a Dutch scholar: would have women learn Latin, 95; portrait, 91.

Excelsior, Longfellow's poem, 123.

Flag, The, PARABLE VIII., 73; American national flag called the Stars and Stripes, 73, or the Star-Spangled Banner, 74, or the Red, White and Blue, 75; not the Flag of the Free till 1865, 78; raised over American public schools, 73; denied to American free-traders, 89; a flag for each nation, 74; the pirate's flag, 75.

Florence, in Italian *Firenze*, 53.

Flower-viewing, in Japan, 183.

France, Revolution of 1789, 26; Republic abolishes slavery in San Domingo, 125; a country of fine roads, 88; French proverb, 119.

Frankfort, in German *Frankfurt-am-Main*, 53.

Franklin, Benjamin (1706–1790), an American philosopher and statesman: would make scholars of women, 95; helped by Cotton Mather's Essays, 155; draws down lightning with a kite, 156; his Autobiography, 155.

Fugitive Slave Law, passed in August, 1850, 77; in accordance with Constitutional provision, 57.

Genoa, in Italian *Genova*, 53.

Germany, famous for its learning, 88; streets swept by women, 98.

Ghent, in French-Belgian *Gand*, 53.

Gibraltar, a Spanish rock held as a fortress by England, 163; view of, 161.

Giotto (1276–1337), Italian painter and architect: his round O, 23.

Glaciers, moving ice-fields, 173; plastic, 144.

Gladstone, William Ewart (born 1809), an English statesman, 105.

INDEX 205

Goodyear, Charles (1800-1860), American inventor of the art of vulcanizing india-rubber, 157.
Great Lakes, Superior, Michigan, Huron, Erie and Ontario, 88.
Greece, ancient, women not allowed to act, 96; Socrates put to death, 165; Alexander, general, 143, 164; beautiful statuary, 148, and temples, 175; modern Greece conquered by Turks, 175.
Guido Reni (1575-1642), Italian painter, 65.
Gulliver, Lemuel, his "Travels" among the Houyhnhnms, 13, the Lilliputians, 163, 164, in Brobdingnag, 164.
Gunpowder, invented first by Chinese, 165; explosion at Leyden in 1807, and in the Parthenon at Athens in 1687, 175.
Gutenberg, John (1397-1468), inventor of printing (about 1450), 133, 136; statue and square in Mainz, 133, 139.

Half-Moon, Henry Hudson's ship, 28.
Hampton, Virginia, negro and Indian school, 148.
Hanover, in German *Hannover*, 53.
Hapsburg, a royal Austrian family, 195.
Harlem River, boundary of Manhattan Island, 87.
Harvard College, founded 1638, 139; President Mather, 138.
Heredity, PARABLE XX., 193.
Hindus, wonderful architecture of, 166.
Holland, native country of Erasmus, 95; refuge of Pilgrim Fathers, 83.
Hook and Hookey, cant terms for *steal* and *truancy*, 55.
Hopkins, Oceanus, born on the *Mayflower* (1620), died in infancy, 84.
Horses, fable of Horse, Stag and Man, Gulliver's island of talking horses, 13; dumb beasts, 14; protected against cruelty by a Society, 13, 17; capable of thinking, 14; milkman's horse, 14; clergyman's horse, 15; circus horse, 17; five-toed horses, 17; horse's skeleton like man's, 18; horses well trained, 18; subject to panic and stampeding, 45.
Hudson, Henry (died 1611), English navigator: discovers the Hudson or North River, 28.

Hudson or **North River**, bounds Manhattan Island on the west, 87; named for its discoverer, 28; its beauty, 28, 29.

India, wonderful ancient architecture, 166; terrible famines, 185.
Indiana, a free State, 168.
Indians, stampede horses, 45; dislike to have portraits taken, 137, 139; capable of civilization, 147; change of looks under education, 196.
Industry, various kinds of, 58; how "protected" in the United States, 59.
Insanity, from deranged organs, 103, 104; from fever, 109; from drunkenness, 106; from indigestion, rage and fear, 108.
Insatiable Mind, PARABLE XII., 113.
Ireland, potato famine (1846-1847), 75.
Italy, ruled by Marcus Aurelius, 198; religious persecution of the Waldenses, 125; famous for its fine art, 88; time told from one to twenty-four o'clock, 103; Revolution of 1848 against Austria, 124, 129; capital Rome, 136.

Japan, flower festivals, 183.
Jinn, an invisible spirit, 153.
John Bull, nickname for England, 65.
John-James and the walnut tree, 34.

Kansas, scene of first armed conflict between North and South (1856), 78.
Kentucky, a former Southern slave State, birthplace of Lincoln, 167, 168.
Kindness to Animals, PARABLE II., 13.

Labor and **Capital**, 69.
Lake Superior, shores abound in copper, 59.
Lamb, Mary (1764-1847), sister of Charles Lamb: poem quoted, 116.
Leghorn, in Italian *Livorno*, 53.
Leyden, a Rhine city, 175.
Lilliputians, little people visited by Gulliver, 163, 164.

Lincoln, Abraham (1809-1865), sixteenth President of the United States: born in Kentucky, 167; his parents, 167; boyhood poverty, 167; taken to Indiana, 167, 168; a tall man (6 feet 4 inches), 165; statesman, 105; abolishes slavery, 79, 168.

Lion of Lucerne, 26; picture of, 21.

Lone Pine, Oregon, destruction of the, 5.

Longfellow, Henry Wadsworth (1807-1882), American poet: poem quoted, 123.

Lucerne, the monument to the Swiss guards, 26.

Lydia, the country of King Crœsus, 176.

Lyons, in French *Lyon*, 54.

Mainz, Rhine city, seat of invention of printing, 53, 133; Gutenberg Square, 133, and statue, 139; view of the city, 131.

Manhattan Island, site of New York city, 87.

Marcus Aurelius Antoninus (121-180), Roman Emperor: good examples from his parents, 198; wars in Egypt, 198, 199; religious "Thoughts," 198, 199.

Marseilles, in French *Marseille*, 54.

Massachusetts, a free State, 77; its bay, 173.

Mather, Cotton (1663-1728), Puritan clergyman of Boston, son of Increase: his "Essays to Do Good," 155.

Mather, Increase (1639-1723), Puritan clergyman of Boston: superstitious, 138.

Mayence, French name for Mainz, 53, 133.

Mayflower, Pilgrim ship (1620), 83.

Mentz, in German *Mainz*, in French *Mayence*, 53, 133.

Mexican War (1846-1848), 85; thought unpatriotic to oppose it, 86.

Mexico, attacked and despoiled by the United States, 85, 86.

Michelangelo Buonarroti (1475-1564), Italian painter, sculptor, architect, 65; picture of his "Twilight and Dawn," 61.

Milan, in Italian *Milano*, 53.

Milton, John (1608-1674), English poet: poem quoted, 64.

Mississippi River, admired by foreigners, 88.
Mob, The, PARABLE V., 43; cholera mobs in Paris, 46.
Monkeys, resemblance to man, 18, 163.
Moon, spoken of as *she*, 63.
Morse, Samuel Finley Breese (1791-1872), American inventor of the electric telegraph, 156.
Mountains, wearing down of, 173; view of the Matterhorn, 121, of Gibraltar, 161.
Munich, in German *München*, 53.

Names, PARABLE VI., 53.
Naples, in Italian *Napoli*, 53; beautiful bay, 54.
Napoleon Bonaparte (1768-1821), general, and Emperor of the French, 105, 164; a little man, 164; puts Toussaint to death, 125, 129; loses an army in Russia, 178; dies on St. Helena, 178.
New England's early superstitions, 138; first printing-office (1639), 139.
New Jersey, half as large as Switzerland, 33.
Niagara Falls, at the eastern end of Lake Erie, 88.
North River, same as Hudson River, 87.
Notre Dame de Paris, church of, 47; view of, 41.

Ohio River, separated free and slave States, 167.
Omar Khayyám (1025-1133), Persian poet: quoted, 143.
Oregon, story of the Lone Pine, 5.
Ozymandias, a fabled king, 179.

Paine, Thomas (1739-1809), English patriot and philanthropist: his motto, 89.
Palisades, cliffs of the Hudson River, 28; a great curiosity to foreigners, 29.
Panza, Sancho, Don Quixote's serving-man, 98, 105; very ignorant, 106, but of a sound mind, 105, 106; governor of an island, 98.
Paris, on the River Seine, 47; church of Notre Dame, 47; cholera times, 46; signs on omnibuses, 113.

INDEX

Parma, earthquake of 1222, 94.
Parthenon, an ancient Athenian temple, 175; view of, 171; sculptured horse from, 11.
Patriotism, PARABLE IX., 83; the real, 88, 89; the false, 85, 86; not to be decided by majorities or boundaries, 87.
Pennsylvania, Carlisle school for Indians, 148.
Persia, the country of King Cyrus, 177; attacked by Crœsus, 177, 178.
Personification, PARABLE VII., 63.
Peschiera, an Italian town and scene of battle, 129.
Pilgrim Fathers, home in Leyden, 175; number sailing for America in 1620, 83; land on Plymouth Rock, 173.
Pitcher-plant, its animal food, 115.
Plasticity, PARABLE XV., 143; plasticity of all substances, 144, especially of organic things, 145.
Plymouth Rock, an erratic boulder, landing-place of the Pilgrims in 1620, 173.
Poetry quoted (first lines):
    Ah! not for idle hatred, not, 126.
    And in thy right hand lead with thee, 64.
    A rose By any other name, 54.
    A traveller from an antique land, 179.
    A youngster at school, more sedate than the rest, 48.
    Each one must do his best, and all endure, 129.
    Every night and every morn, 186.
    For I remember stopping by the way, 143.
    Hast thou named all the birds without a gun? 8.
    Imperious Cæsar, dead, and turned to clay, 143.
    I saw a boy with eager eye, 116.
    Leaves have their time to fall, 184.
    Long have I lasted in this world, 'tis true, 188.
    Not failure, but low aim, is crime, 126.
    Of old sat Freedom on the heights, 64.
    She sprang no fatal leak, 64.
    Some are but weeds, 169.
    Sport that wrinkled Care derides, 64.
    Steal not this book for fear of shame, 36.

The Moon doth with delight, 63.
There, in the twilight cold and gray, 123.
The woman's cause is man's; they rise or sink, 99.
Toussaint, the most unhappy man of men, 125.
Uncle Sam is rich enough to give us all a farm, 67.
Where lies the land to which yon Ship must go? 63.
Where Toil shall call the charmer Health his bride, 65.
Woodman, spare that tree, 5.

Postage-stamp, the first, 65.

Printing, invented by Chinese, 165; where and by whom invented in Europe, 133; art described, 133; first printing-office in United States (1639), 139.

Property, PARABLE IV., 33; property in water, 35, 36; in books and other articles, 36; not dependent on being marked with owner's name, 36, 37; its destruction robbery, 38, 39.

Protection to American industry, 59; makes us hate foreigners for selling cheap, 89.

Puritans, settle at Salem, Massachusetts, 85; superstitious, 138; not hospitable to poor comers, 169; persecute the Quakers, 125.

Pyramids, royal Egyptian tombs, 193, 199; view of them, 191.

Quakers, persecuted in Massachusetts, 125.
Quixote, Don, a mad Spanish knight errant, 104; a scholar, 106; attacks windmills and flocks of sheep, 104.

Railroad, in French *chemin de fer*, 53.
Rhine, German river running past Mainz, 133, and Leyden, 175; seat of invention of printing, 133; view of the river, 131.

Rocks, disfigured by advertisements, 25, 27; made noble by sculpture, 26.

Rocky Mountains, admired by foreigners, 88; wearing away 174.

Roentgen, Wilhelm Conrad von (born 1845), German inventor (1895) of X-rays photography, 156.

Rome, in Italian *Roma*, 53; capital of Italy, 136; church of St.

Peter's, 54; Romans conquered Great Britain, 60; masters of the world, 148; did not allow women actors, 96.

Romulus and **Remus**, twin brothers, founders of Rome (753 B. C.), 147.

Rousseau, Jean-Jacques (1712-1778), a Swiss writer: story of the walnut tree, 34; portrait, 31.

Royal George, British war-vessel sunk in port August 29, 1782, 64.

Russia, invaded by Napoleon, 178.

Saint Mark's Square, Venice, 103.

Salem, Massachusetts, settlement of the Puritans, 85.

Salimbene, Fra, Italian chronicler: adventure in an earthquake, 94; opinion of man's superiority to woman, 94, 98.

San Domingo, home of Toussaint, 125.

Sanity, PARABLE XI., 103; preserved by care of the body, 107.

Santa Maria, Columbus's ship, 83; picture of her, 81.

School, the house marked by a flag, 73; desks and books disfigured, 23, 24; the teacher a captain, 43; panic in a fire, 44.

Scotland, superstition about portraits, 137.

Seine, River, 47; view of, 41.

Sexes, equality of the, 93.

Shakspere, William (1564-1616), English poet and dramatist, 54, 105; plays quoted, 54, 108, 143; portrait, 51.

Shelley, Percy Bysshe (1792-1822), an English poet, 178; poem quoted, 179.

Ship, called *she* by poets and other folks, 63; alphabet of famous ships, 83, 85.

Silver dollars, worth only fifty cents, 58.

Slavery, soft names for it in the United States Constitution and in the talk of slaveholders, 57; created four classes in the South, 167; cannot live with schools, 79; cause of, and abolished by, the Civil War (1861-1865), 79, 168.

Slaves, brought from Africa to the United States, 57; counted with freemen in the South for representation in Congress, 56; word kept out of the Constitution, 57; fugitive slaves to be caught and sent back, 57, 77; a million slaves in 1808, 77.

Slave trade, African, horrors of, 76; trade allowed by Constitution till 1808, then piracy, 76; word kept out of the Constitution, 57.
Socrates (470–399 B. C.), Greek philosopher, 165.
Solon (638-559 B. C.), a lawgiver of Athens: adventure with Crœsus, 176.
State, The, what it consists of, 69.
Story, of Anthony Burns made a slave again, 77; Crœsus, Solon and Cyrus, 176; Don Quixote, the windmills and the sheep, 104; Excelsior, 123; Fra Salimbene and the earthquake, 94; Giotto's round O, 23; Horse, the Stag and the Man, 13; Horse who knew when Sunday came, 15; John-James and the walnut tree, 33; Lone Pine, 5; Men turned into trees, 9; Merchant and Jinn, 153; Poisoners in Paris, 46; Rousseau and the walnut tree, 33; Sancho Panza at table, 98; Swiss guards massacred, 26; Walnut tree and the willow tree, 33; Washington and his hatchet, 3.
Superstition, PARABLE XIV., 133; various superstitions, 137, 138.
Swiss guards, massacred in Paris, August 10, 1792: monument to, 26.
Switzerland, small size and many languages, 33; Lucerne and its lion monument, 26; Swiss guards in the service of France, 26.

Tahitians, a dark-skinned people of the South Pacific Ocean, 166.
Tenderness for Living Things, PARABLE I., 3.
Tennyson, Alfred (1809-1892), English poet: poem quoted, 64; "The Princess" quoted, 99.
Tiber, river on which Rome is situated, 136.
Toussaint L'Ouverture (1743-1803), murdered by Napoleon, 125, 129.
Trees, longevity of, 6, 184; Washington chops down a cherry tree, 3; destruction of the Lone Pine, 5; good reasons for destroying trees, 8; English laws forbidding advertisements on them, 27.

INDEX

Truancy, called *hookey*, 55.
Turin, in Italian *Torino*, 53.
Turks, take Constantinople, 136, and conquer Greece, 175.

Uncle Sam, nickname for United States, 65; robbed by Americans, 67.
United States, called Columbia and Uncle Sam and Brother Jonathan, 65; Civil War (1861-1865), 78.

Vandalism, PARABLE III., 23.
Venice, in Italian *Venezia*, 53; a city of canals, 54; clock in St. Mark's Square, 103; war with the Turks in Greece, 175.
Venus, a Greek goddess: statue found on the island of Melos, 149.
Vertebrates, animals having a backbone, 18.
Vesuvius, volcano of, 54.
Vicissitude, PARABLE XVIII., 173.
Virginia, Natural Bridge, 29; the slave Anthony Burns escapes from Virginia, 77; carried back from Boston, 78; Virginia the last seat of the Civil War, 78; Hampton school for negroes and Indians, 148.

Wagner, Richard (1813-1883), a German musical composer, 105.
Washington, George (1732-1799), general, and first President of the United States: chops down his father's cherry tree, 3; a tall man (6 feet 2 inches), 165; climbs the Natural Bridge of Virginia, 29; President of a slaveholding country, 79.
West India Islands, 125.
Witches, former belief in, 138, 139.
Women, have same faculties as men, 97; not encouraged to become learned, 95; not allowed to act in Greek, Roman and Chinese theatres, 96; not till lately allowed to speak in public or to serve on school committees, 96; not generally allowed now to vote like men, 97; some things allowed them, 97; their interest in good government, 97; chief educators of children, 95; sweep the streets in Germany, 98.

Wordsworth, William (1770-1850), English poet: poems quoted, 63, 125.

Yellowstone Park, between the States of Montana, Wyoming and Idaho, 88.
Yosemite Valley, in California, 88.

www.ingramcontent.com/pod-product-compliance
Lightning Source LLC
Chambersburg PA
CBHW021820230426
43669CB00008B/809